Sweet Tooth

Sweet Tooth

BRIAN B. HAWTHORNE

LitPrime
"Your story is our priority"

LitPrime Solutions
21250 Hawthorne Blvd
Suite 500, Torrance, CA 90503
www.litprime.com
Phone: 1-800-981-9893

Published by LitPrime Solutions   10/19/2022

ISBN: 979-8-88703-064-7(sc)
ISBN: 979-8-88703-065-4(hc)
ISBN: 979-8-88703-066-1(e)

Library of Congress Control Number: 2022917197

Books by Brian B. Hawthorne

<u>Outlandish!</u> Fairhome, a world isolated in space and time, where women rule, and men -- there are none! Just a poor but useful substitute...

<u>The Day of Magic Rain</u> Change has come to Fairhome. But is the Race of Women ready to rejoin the Human Race?

<u>Action!</u> A tale that mind-bendingly mixes everyday reality with science fictional unreality, as the Future comes to the Present!

<u>Reaction!</u> ... Would you like to go back and live your life over? Be young again? Live for a very long time? -- Are you *sure?*

<u>Ethereal</u> When Cthulhu's Cousin moves in next door, things are likely to change in the neighborhood – and they do!

<u>Evelynish</u> This is a story of broken people, trying on their own to find a way to fit into society without being ground up even further. Can that work? Could that possibly work? Broken people can't fit in. They just fall into places where they can't fall any more. They just -- come to rest there.

<u>Sweet Tooth</u> Dani's father works at Genano, a genetic manipulation enterprise where they can help you become the person you want to be. – Be careful what you wish for!

<u>Our Side of The Wall</u>: Patriotic and Inspirational Poetry from an Unusual Perspective -- My job as a poet, to let you see the *other* other side.

Contents

0

Introduction: Time-Skips and Flashbacks

(Saturday Evening, April 22, 2119)
Timeline: __|_____

Blake Corrigan looked from his view of the sunset into his drink. Idly he swirled it around.

"I've been thinking."

Rho glanced over and shifted one foot on top of the other. "Should I fasten my seat-belt?"

His smile flickered for just an instant. "Maybe. Let me preface my remarks by saying I'm not upset with, disappointed with, or unhappy about anybody, but I've come to the conclusion that we're missing a body or two."

"I have no idea what you're talking about. Are you secretly a serial murderer and someone has discovered part of your stash?"

"No, it isn't that." He took a deep breath, and let part of it out. "By this time in my life, I thought I might have a grandchild or two."

"Oh. Harvey was showing vacation photos?"

"You read my mind too well. That's why I gave up the serial murdering years ago. No, I've just always thought it would be fun to have a little girl around to dress up and tell her she's pretty."

"You can take me shopping anytime you want, you know."

"I don't think you would be interested in pinafores and tutus."

"You're really serious? You want to be responsible for a small child?"

"Yeah, I think I do. Years ago, I had a picture in my mind about what I would be doing when I reached certain milestones. I guess I was thinking about a granddaughter."

"Well, that doesn't seem likely any time soon. I don't think Dani is ready for fatherhood."

Blake glanced over his shoulder. "Say, Dani!"

The couple's son came out from the kitchen. "Yes, Dad?"

"Are you ready to be a father?"

Dani was a meter and a half tall, just under five feet, and weighed forty-two kilograms. He was a trim and athletic ninety pounds. Dusty and soiled from a just-completed baseball game, he fit the profile precisely for a healthy ten-year-old boy.

He seemed to consider the question.

"I suppose I *could*, but I don't think I would be a very good father. I haven't really thought about it much."

Blake set his glass down carefully. He gestured to his son to come closer, and wrapped his arms around him. Blake looked into his son's eyes. "One more question then. Are you happy? Really happy?"

Dani smiled. "Yes, Dad. I'm very happy. Everything's just perfect."

Blake smiled.

"Go get ready for your bath, Dani." Rho told him.

Dani kissed his father and went back into the kitchen.

"Well, I suppose that leaves Plan B then." Rho said.

"Whatever is Plan B?"

"I could get pregnant again."

Blake nearly spilled his drink. "Say that again?"

"I could get pregnant."

"You'd do that?"

"Why not? It wasn't so bad with Dani, and second births are said to be easier."

"That was a long time ago."

Rho stared at him challengingly, "I dare you to tell me I look a day over thirty."

"Uh, no thanks. It's a long way down. I hope you don't think I maneuvered you into this."

"I've known you had something on your mind. Would it surprise you to hear that I have thought about this myself?"

"A little. You seem pretty occupied with Dani. I thought you might not want to take on too much."

"Piffle! Dani's no trouble. He'd be a big help to me if I had a little one to care for. It's not like he would have to take time off from his job."

"True. He'd have time if he wanted to help."

"Oh, you know he would! He's so full of life and energy! When he says he's happy, I just get thrills up my spine, knowing that it's absolutely true!"

"Well, this conversation didn't quite go the way I thought it would, but I'm pleased with the direction it took."

"I guess we'd better get ready for some changes. That will be novel! Right now, I'm going to check on Dani. I thought I saw some dried blood on his knee." She put her magazine down and went back inside.

A few minutes later Blake went into the house with his glass. Idly, he considered filling it again, but that would be less than useless. Flavor aside, there just wasn't much point to booze. He followed voices to the bathroom where Rho was shampooing Dani's hair.

Rho smiled. "You guys never keep your hair clean enough. You wouldn't shampoo once a month if I didn't get after you about it."

"You have to do it that often? Who knew?" Blake answered.

Dani laughed. Rho rinsed the soap off him and had him stand up. "I was right about the blood. Dani told me he had skinned his knee again. Look at it now."

Blake looked at him. Dani wiped the water from his eyes and smiled back.

"Which leg?" asked Blake.

"That's my point. It's completely healed."

"We have a good insurance policy." Blake said, and went off to his den while Rho toweled Dani dry.

It *was* a good insurance policy. He reviewed how it had come about. Blake's career had landed him with the premier nanotech genetic

3

engineering firm in the country, Genano Health, Incorporated. Not only had it profited him handsomely, but his family had also benefited from the developments as they came out.

Dani was really the first to do so in any large way. As he was moving forward in life, some of the advanced, and *very* expensive, developments coming out of the labs got a trial run in his growing body.

One of the first was a simple locating function. Tied into his inner ear, and functioning on a microscopic scale unknown to earlier researchers, tiny micro-mechanical and optical devices helped him to orient himself to a planetary coordinate system. The same upgrade made him a beacon to the appropriate searchers. It was not only impossible for him to get lost; it was also impossible for him to <u>be</u> lost.

Then there was the communication entity, masquerading as an installed tooth. As a means of explaining its functioning to the boy, he was given the impression that a tooth was being implanted to replace one he lost. He named the entity Sweet Tooth.

Sweet Tooth was an internal communication system. It could send and receive messages, and be controlled by sub-vocal commands issued by the boy. He could speak to it, and it could respond to him, without anyone knowing such communication was happening.

Extending from this capability, computer research channels allowed Dani to investigate avenues of increasing interest to him as he came to further maturity. Soon it was difficult to determine whether information requested from him came from his own previous knowledge, or from his access to a digitized world.

Once this capability had advanced to its ultimate levels, Dani's official education had come to an end. He was no longer required to go to school.

That was when he was eight years old.

Idly, Blake mixed another drink.

* * *

(Monday, March 11, 2109)
Timeline: |_____

Blake returned home one evening with some exciting news; a method had been developed to build a genetic "firewall".

"What ever are you talking about?" Rho asked him.

"We've developed a technique to directly repair most physical body damage, and even genetic damage that comes about through cosmic radiation, chemical exposure, and the operations of free radicals inside your body."

Rho looked at him. "And that means?"

"Well, basically it means that we may be able to throw away our band-aids. With a pattern to follow, the body can summon its defenses to repair an injury at almost lightning speed. We will have a new weapon in the war against cancer and aging, too. Our research indicates that people who undergo the treatment may be for all practical purposes immunized against many forms of cancer and some of the causes of aging."

"That sounds like what your people have been working toward for ages! How does it work?"

"It was a surprisingly simple breakthrough; basically just a change in the way we looked at the problem. It may help if you know something about holograms. A holographic exposure, when illuminated by laser light, displays the scene that was photographed."

"What's interesting is that if you cut the hologram film in half, you don't lose half the image. You just get a slightly degraded image. You can cut the film to a fraction of its original size and still get an image."

"That degradation of the holographic information is similar to what happens in the body as cells age and reproduce, and error is introduced. Each new generation is like a cut in the hologram."

"What we did was to give the nanobots a holographic memory. When they are scanning your genome and physical structure for damage, they compare it to nine other scan events. We call it holographic stacking. It's the equivalent of putting the holographic exposure back together."

"Is it safe?"

"It's safer than aspirin. We're looking at cell cultures that have gone through twenty generations without developing the kind of signal degradation that you normally get. That means some tissues may last twenty times their normal lifespan. Imagine a human heart two thousand years old!"

"Oh, my! What have you wrought?"

"Well, it's a revved-up repair system. We're calling our procedure cellular holography, and it's a big step. It's a way of taking an image of your body gestalt. Then your body works to maintain itself against that standard. In an unmodified tissue, changes occur without their having any kind of compass to direct them home. Cells end up literally not knowing up from down. It's no wonder we get old and die; we lose our way."

"Are you saying we can get this treatment? That it would be a way to protect us from accident and injury?"

"That's exactly what I'm saying. It's like the difference between the response of professionals in an emergency room, and the way injuries used to be treated in the Napoleonic Wars!"

"You and I will go in next week to get the cellular imaging done. Then they'll start developing the unique nanobots that each of us will require. In about half a year, our bodies will each carry their own emergency room!"

Her radiant smile suddenly faded. "Wait a minute! You and I? What about Dani?"

Blake grew serious too. "Well, they would be reluctant to give him the treatment now. He's still growing up. We're not sure what might happen, but there's a chance he would stop growing. If his internal regulators see that his image clock has reached a stopping point, they might go into stasis and stop feeding out growth hormones and other chemical signals."

"You're worried that the body image will get frozen at the time of treatment? But only if you get the treatment can you be protected from serious injury?"

"I wouldn't describe it that way, but I think you've got the gist of it."

"Tell me something. Right now, if Dani were to suffer, say, a ruptured spleen in a sports injury, he could likely die. But if he had this treatment, what would be the best case scenario?"

"A ruptured spleen? Hmm. I'm going on pure conjecture at this point, but if his new nanobots would work the way they were described to me, they would immediately stop the internal blood loss, suture the injury site, and begin regrowing the damaged tissues, harvesting the good cells and scavenging materials from the damaged ones. He'd probably just need to take it easy for a few hours, and then he'd be as good as new the next day."

"Well then, we absolutely *must* get him into the program as well. We can't take a chance on losing him, even a remote chance."

"But Rho, the way I understand it, that would give Dani's repair devices a picture of him as he is right now. When his bones start trying to grow longer, that might be interpreted as an injury site, and his growth stopped before it could begin. We might well stunt his growth."

She turned away from him. "Oh, I don't know what would be best! I have known as a mother that eventually I must lose Dani, either to accident or illness or to his growing older and apart from us. Either of those possibilities would just tear me apart! I love him so much exactly the way he is right now! I don't know …"

She turned back to look at him. "If I could preserve that, capture that image, and give him a long, long childhood, while keeping him safe from injury … oh what a wonderful thing it would be for him, and what a dear, dear delight it would be for me as well."

"A boy frozen in time? Watching his classmates grow older and move along with their lives, while he stays at home, or runs around in the park, like the only boy on an island?"

"Like Peter Pan?" Rho searched his eyes. "Every morning, when I see him, I think, these are the days I should treasure; they will be so fleeting. I wonder what *he* might say? You spoke of his classmates, but I think that was only a figure of speech. He *has* no classmates! He has only the friends he finds of the day, for the games of the day. That is his life. Would it be wrong for it to be a long one?"

Blake was taken aback. He really hadn't stopped to consider the effect of this development as applied to Dani. What exactly was his life destined to be, now that they had already interfered with it? Even now, there were things forever barred to him in a normal childhood; the fear of getting lost, and the joy of successfully meeting challenges with only his own resources. He would never know those things. If he came to adulthood without them, what kind of person would he be?

Blake thought about smug, self-important people he had known; those who had all the answers, and could never be shaken or bargained with. Was that what he had made of his son?

He sensed that Rho was adamant about this point, and that she would not accept a change that did not include all of them fully.

He pulled his wife into an embrace.

"You may be right. It certainly wouldn't surprise me to discover that I am wrong. Maybe we should just explain the matter to Dani, and either all go through it, or none of us."

* * *

(Saturday, April 22, 2119)
Timeline: __|_____

Blake looked into his drink and remembered with a start the emotionalism of that moment. Perhaps emotions had driven Rho to her position. Maybe Dani's empathy with her had led him in the direction she wanted him to go.

But he himself, as the father, should have been able to use rationality to steer his course. He knew that the procedure was experimental, and that it presented the risk of altering his son's normal development.

The problem was that, then as well as now, he could not predict what kind of man Dani would become. That was his excuse.

Having health and long life was a blessing. Desiring it, to the point that he let his wife be the scapegoat for his actions, was his curse. A blessing and a curse in the same magic elixir. The way of things.

He looked again at his notes and diary entries with their dates, their damnable dates, for the monumental changes he had too willingly foisted on his own son, and the results that had come about for his family.

For them, it had been a terribly short ten years. The daily routines had merged into a seamless chain of repetitious trivialities and delights.

His sweet little Dani, the loving energetic child who had kissed his father an hour ago, was now twenty years old.

1

Go with me to a party?...
Sun 25 May 2142

(Sunday, May 25, 2142)
Timeline: _____|_____

Dani sat down at the base of a tree. The soft moss accepted him like a comfortable armchair.

"Is everyone here?" he thought.

"We're all here, Dani. What did you want?"

"I don't know. I'm bored."

"Would you like to have a picnic? We could have fried chicken, sweet peas, watermelon …"

"No. I'm not hungry, Sweet Tooth. I think I'm just bored."

A curious squirrel hopped over and looked up at him. Accommodatingly, Dani reached out and petted it like a cat.

Dani was forty-three years old, and he wore the body of a ten-year old child. He had many playmates who looked much the same. Most of them were probably ten years old in actuality.

For the things that he liked to do, this body shape was suitable. It had a good combination of strength and agility, balance and coordination that could be used tirelessly in active games or other activities. Because he lived in a society in which employment was more for entertainment than for any other purpose, being able to occupy himself in play was important to his mental health. At least that's what he told himself constantly.

When he had first begun approaching the teenage years, the gangling awkwardness that he saw in others disturbed him, and he had turned away from it, preferring to remain what had become most comfortable for him. Now, his diminished bulk and stature was as much a part of his personality as his cheerful sense of humor and friendly nature.

Personal emancipation came early to young people in Dani's society. The early introduction of cybernetic implants for health and safety monitoring, educational bootstrapping, communications and private entertainment, and for other purposes, gave individuals a phenomenal range of personal control over processes that once followed a set and invariable time schedule.

One of the first variations from historical trends was in the onset of the menstrual cycle in young ladies. After it became possible to delay this often upsetting change of life, many parents and their charges came to agree that such a delay was really in the best interests of the child.

A long period of hormonal manipulation had caused a general impression that girls were being forced to mature too quickly, and that slowing that process was a means of swinging the pendulum back to what had supposedly been more normal. The emphasis on the joy and innocence of childhood had a philosophical rekindling. His mother had been an early adopter of *that*.

This, of course, had opened the floodgates for those who felt that childhood did not last long enough anyway, and such an opening was perhaps even taken to extremes by some parents who delighted in having children, but only as long as they were small and cute. One could see a similar tendency in the treatment and breeding of small dogs in previous centuries.

In any case, Dani had chosen, with his parents' blessing, to forestall his development for the indefinite future, but that decision did not hinder his ability to act in the wider social sphere. Even at ten, he was considered virtually an adult. His parents could be watchful from a distance, and they seemed to feel that distance was strengthening for him.

Dani could walk around the world if he chose. The sights were there for the sightseeing. Or he could "travel", if that was the appropriate word, say to Paris to look at the reconstructed Eiffel Tower, or to the Great Wall of China, by simply entering a chamber and being whisked along without any sensation of motion to his destination.

During his long childhood, Dani had explored his neighborhood, his city, his local countryside, and traveled farther and farther in quest of new things to see and do.

From time to time, this produced the conditions for a bit of ennui and lassitude. At the moment, for example, there wasn't anything he couldn't do, and so there wasn't anything he wanted to do. He was bored. He might just sit here for a week.

His sister appeared in front of him. Lori was twenty-three, and she looked it, with pert breasts and an all-over tan.

"Would you like to go with me to a party?"

"Okay." He wasn't bored any more.

Lori helped him up and brushed off his shorts from invisible dust. Helpfully, Dani brushed off her bikini-clad derriere in return.

Holding his hand, she walked with him to a transport station. Inside the chamber, she held him on her lap and stroked his brow and cheek. Lori was a head taller than her brother, and half again his weight. As far as she was concerned, that made him her little brother. A decade or so before, they had been exactly the same height and weight.

"You're my favorite brother."

"I'm your only brother."

"Well, then, you're my favorite something."

Dani thought about it. Here and now, beauty was as common as clothing. Anyone could change his appearance at will. Relationships were not the way they used to be, once upon a time.

Historical information was available to them, of course. The way people used to live was known in the same way that it was known that travel once meant living in sailing vessels as they were blown about by the winds and storms. People of his time could envision it, and they could observe recreations, but the reality was quite beyond their imagining.

At Lori's apartment, she insisted on bathing him, so that he could then bathe her. Cleanliness was one of her personality quirks, as was her slight tendency to mother him.

Like his mother, she looked at his boyish exterior, and reacted to that, even though she knew that he was old enough to be her father. That tendency on the part of women was one of his better reasons for keeping the boyish form.

When Lori was much younger, about four, he had changed to being a girl so they could be best friends. He had been twenty-four at the time, with the body of a ten-year old boy, but he had physically become a ten-year old girl for fourteen years, remaining unmodified otherwise while Lori grew up. Then six years ago he had changed back to being the ten-year old boy he had always been, and always wanted to be.

The interlude of being a girl had not interfered with his social connections. He still had gone out to play sports, ride bikes, roller skate, and other physically demanding activities. Those times when he and his friends were naked together, as at parties or for swimming, having boy parts was merely another thing to be teased about.

For now, his body image was "imprinted" on his genome pattern, marking it as the norm to which all processes operated. After close to forty years of it, he had become psychologically imprinted on it as well.

Dani's parents had a strange, or perhaps strained, existence. His mother treated him as though she never expected him to change in any way, and his father always seemed to look at him as if he were waiting for him to do it.

Dani suspected it was because he felt guilt for having stuck him with the body of a ten-year old. If drinking were an outlet for his misgivings, his father would have been an alcoholic.

Fortunately or unfortunately, the genetic treatment his family had undergone, (even Lori, just recently), prevented alcohol from having the reaction that it might in others. His father buried himself in work, and enjoyed the separation time from his family.

The masquerade had brought the siblings very close together indeed.

From early on, Dani had been left in charge of the child for days at a time. It wasn't long before they were inseparable.

Lori shared her heart and soul with him on a continual basis. He had always been her diary, and her confessor. It never occurred to her that he was unworthy of trust or could hurt her in any way. He was her dearest friend, and she was his dear friend also.

Dani reflected on those past moments as he washed her delectable body. His transition into maleness had not been a problem in their relationship. Lori accepted his change as she had accepted the changes in her own body, and the previous changelessness of his.

He had been bigger, then he was the same, then he was smaller, and then finally he became a boy. She didn't care. She had grown up laughing and cuddling and sleeping with him, and she hoped never to lose him.

After the bathing, she teased him about his childlike features for a moment. Then Lori held him close, and still, and kissed him seriously.

"I have loved you every way that it is possible to do, have I not?"

"I think so. I don't know what we could have left out."

"Good. I couldn't think of anything. I considered starting over, just to make sure."

"It might take a while. I thought you had a party to go to."

She traced along his skin with her fingers and kissed his eyes. "Oh, there are always parties, but we could do this later too."

Dani stretched. "Ready when you are. I'm not busy."

"That's what makes you perfect."

"Perfect in what way?"

"You're always available."

"Oh. I thought you meant I was a perfect lover."

Lori laughed and kissed him again.

"You aren't even a very good lover. But I love you more than anyone else."

"You don't mean that."

"That I love you more?"

"No. That I'm not a good lover."

"That's true. You're actually a very special lover. But when I make love to you, I think about making you happy. When I'm with someone else, I can ignore them and concentrate on myself." Lori said thoughtfully.

"It isn't pride on my part. It's just that I know your body better than you know it yourself, and being a girl for fourteen years taught me things about that as well."

She kissed him again. "You're right. You're a doctor of love. When we get to the party, I'm going to have you as a sleeping partner."

"Sleeping?"

"Yes. I've met a fascinating researcher. He's only fourteen years old, but he's a genius, and he still has to sleep every night. Tomorrow, after the party, he wants to make an announcement, so everyone is sleeping over."

"Well, that's different."

"I knew you'd like it!" She ran her fingers over his body again. "We can start the lovemaking over again tonight. I remember the first time. Do you?"

"Of course! I was female then, though."

"We'll improvise."

He kissed her.

"All right, then. Let's get ready. You can paint my costume on me. You're good at that, too!"

She chose to leave her hair alone, but he painted her body as a leather-clad adventuress. The illusion was transformative. Even up close your eye would perceive clothing, although it was purely illusion. Lori was comfortable in her skin, whatever the company.

The design went on quickly, as it was mostly the same dark color, with silver highlights of buckles and snaps. In just a few minutes, Lori was ready for her party.

For his own costume, Dani chose a doctor's tunic and some comfortable lined meshmetal shorts and boots.

Holding his hand again, Lori led them to a transport chamber, and pulled him onto her lap once more. This trip was longer, and it was full evening where they arrived. (Sunday, May 25, 2142)

The house was a large mountain retreat, with a magnificent view of a peaceful valley and sleepy hamlet nestled under towering snow-capped peaks. A quilt-work of fields blanketed the valley.

Lori strode into the middle of things as if she owned the place. Dani tagged along at her side.

She found their host, one Malcolm, surrounded by a throng of admirers. Lori hugged him, receiving a friendly pat on her rump in the process.

"Malcolm, sweetie! This is my brother, Dani Corrigan."

Malcolm shook hands with him. "I'm so glad you could come, Lori! Make yourself at home. You'll have the eleventh bedroom, up on the second level and to the right, marked 11B. Your brother?"

"He'll stay with me. He's my doctor."

"Of course. Welcome! Have some treats. We have the thousand cheese table, and an equal number of wines and synthmeats."

After a time, they separated. Dani found a stringed instrument musical group, and sat in on viola. The group was talented, and he noticed they had a few fans clustered around. Musical talent was commonly developed around the world, and in a crowd this size, more than half were likely to have it. He synced in effortlessly.

Lori circulated, refreshing and building her circle of international acquaintances. Soon he saw that a would-be Lothario had attached himself to her. Dani smiled. Lori liked accessorizing, and the dark-haired dancer made a good match for the moment.

Later in the evening, Lori brought him over to meet Dani. The exchange was pleasant, but Lori somehow let slip that she would have to leave early to put her brother to bed, and shortly her companion took his reluctant leave of her.

When he saw her dancing alone several minutes later, she winked at him.

Soon the party was winding down, and they made their goodbyes and departed.

Their bedroom had a view window also, although it was obviously replicated. Dani took his clothes off and stood drinking in the scene across the valley. The lights from the village looked merry and inviting, and the snow peaks seemed to glow.

Lori stepped up behind him and pulled him into a caress, stroking his chest and stomach.

"I'm going to shower now."

He had expected that. "Do you want help?"

"No, I'll just be a minute. Wait for me."

Dani pulled up a small divan chair and sat forward on it, bringing his legs up akimbo. He assessed the various flavors he had eaten and consumed during the evening, filing them away with the help of his cybernetic implants. Two dozen distinctive voices shared his brain and body, assisting him with such mundane tasks as body maintenance, health and safety, locating him in space and tracking where he had been or wanted to be, and letting him know where other things and other people were.

It was such a device that had let Lori find him in the park. She could as well have sent him a message with the equivalent of telepathy, but that had lately been considered to be a rudeness. People often liked being alone with their thoughts. Having a voice go off unbidden in your head could be distracting and a nuisance.

The privacy of your thoughts was in this day more important than physical privacy, which was an irrelevancy.

Lori came out, fresh and clean once more. She took up a position behind him on the chair, and pulled him against her. Bending her own legs around him, she straightened his legs out. Dani relaxed his head against her soft breasts, and let his arms fall to his sides.

Lori began tracing her fingertips gently along his temples, and down his throat, then across his chest and stomach, slowly caressing him from top to bottom.

"I was thinking. For our first time, you were big and older, and I was young and smaller. So this time around, I'll play you, and you can play me."

"You're going to *play* me?"

Lori caressed him in a particular spot. "Yes."

"For our first time, you didn't have to do anything except lie still." Dani responded.

"So lie still."

"Well, I don't mind that, but you were a girl and so was I. At the moment, if I am to play you, I am not currently a girl."

"We'll improvise." She leaned down and kissed his cheek. "Be still. You're a very small child, innocent of sex, and I am your older sibling, giving you a loving and tender introduction to its mysteries."

Dani relaxed, trying to get into the mood. His childhood was a seemingly long time ago. He had never gone through anything quite like this, so he was improvising too.

He programmed his body to react to the erogenous stimulation, but not to carry forward beyond that. Ejaculation wasn't necessary in order to achieve orgasm, and would be an unneeded complication for their play. One of the ironic advantages of his cybernetic complexity was that he could be completely asexual, or be a satyr for an extended period.

Lori's hands gently, so gently, explored his limp body, holding him in a loving embrace as she moved her hands over his awakened skin.

For nearly half an hour, his body remained entirely limp, despite the erotic stimulation. Then he modified his internal program, and permitted a reaction to become apparent.

Lori's hands continued their ministrations. Softly, she sang a lullaby love song.

> "Open, my flower. Open to me,
> Letting my touch drink its fill.
> Fill up my senses with perfumes and shivers,
> Adorable blossom, be still ...
>
> Lay still, my darling, close those big eyes,
> Waken the feel of new lands,
> Open your mind to the treasure whose sharing,
> Gently I bring in my hands ..."

Her voice crooned him into a stupor, while her hands hypnotized him into a lethargy of satiety. He felt like a cake, fresh and warm from the oven, to which loving caresses applied a frosting of exquisite delight. This was a game he had never played before.

Lori carried him like a sleepy child to the bed, and arranged his body carefully. She lay down beside him and began kissing and caressing him tenderly. Her lips, her hands, explored his ears, his neck, his tender and ticklish ribs, and all of his body in a careful survey of delight.

Then she began demonstrating for him some of the things she had learned that could be particularly delightful for men, even when they masqueraded as boys.

By morning's light, they had gone through about half of their repertoire of various lovemaking techniques and procedures that they had learned, discovered, or invented.

By mutual consent, they decided to stop, and to lie quietly in each other's arms. They slept. Mon26May2142

Each was thoroughly satiated, and filled with delight once again that they had such a fulfilling relationship. There is no sleep more comforting.

With full sun, they awakened. Dani snuggled his shoulder into the shelter of Lori's arm and reached out to caress her breast. She kissed his lips and patted his bottom at the same time. "What's up, Doc?" She said.

"Not me! I'm going to be down for a while."

She laughed. "Nonsense! You could be up for a week without a problem."

He moved his hand over the curves of her abdomen. "True, but I don't like to attract attention that way. I find it more fun to let people underestimate me."

"I told people you were my doctor."

"It's okay. Your friend is going to make an announcement today. I won't mind if they assume I know what it's about."

"They know you're pretending, anyway. You were good in the band last night."

"Passable. My execution is good, but some people are *really* talented."

"You're a talented love doctor. Maybe I should help you advertise."

"I'll let you know if I see someone I want to be advertised to."

She smiled. "Let's go get cleaned up and decide what we're going to wear."

As they bathed, Dani asked her, "Are you going to keep this shape for a while?" He was soaping up her legs as if washing a racehorse.

"Probably, you?"

"Yeah, I think so. It doesn't bother you, does it?"

She ruffled his hair. "Not at all, lover. You suit me just fine. I might let some of my girlfriends borrow you, though, just to let them see what they've been missing."

He rose, slithering up her body and ending in a kiss. "I suppose I could schedule them into my busy routine."

They rinsed off and dried.

"Have you ever thought about trying to do something special, like Malcolm?"

"Well, it's a competitive field. I do little things from time to time, programming and minor machine design improvements. Our society isn't really geared for much change these days. I guess one problem is that other than my own satisfaction, there's no reason to work very hard at anything. Among other things, Dad has seen to it that neither of us needs to work, yet he still goes in every day."

"I never thought about you working. I thought you didn't."

"It can be hard to tell sometimes. By some definitions, I can be working when I'm sitting alone somewhere."

"I can't think of anything I know how to do that anyone would pay for."

"I can, and it isn't being a love-goddess. You'd make a good hostess at parties like this one. If Malcolm wants to hold more of them, you could plan and coordinate them."

"Hmm. I hadn't thought about that. Speaking of planning and coordination, what shall we wear? Would you want to be a Cupid, with a little quiver of arrows and beautiful white wings? You have a cute butt."

"Thanks, but I don't know if the announcement part is the place for costumes. Besides, Cupid should be even younger and pudgy."

"Not all of them were. You haven't visited the right museums. One I saw looked a lot like you. Maybe I'll take on a job being a hostess, just so I can think of naked costumes you could wear."

" 'Naked costumes' is a contradiction."

"Well, I like the way you look, anyway."

Dani looked down at himself. "That's not the look I'm going for. I'm trying for utilitarian, not sexy."

"I didn't say you looked sexy. I think you just look delicious! I want to eat you up!"

Dani kissed her. "I'll wear some shorts and a polo shirt, and some sneakers."

"Oh, poo! I may as well wear a dress."

"No, I know what you should wear. I'll design it for you." Dani stood lost in thought for a few minutes, and then the delivery chime sounded.

Lori retrieved a package from the delivery panel. It was a miniscule costume that she held in front of her. It was so tiny that she could easily have concealed it in one hand.

"You want me to wear this?"

"Try it on. I'll help you."

Other than paint, this was probably the skimpiest costume that Lori had ever considered wearing. Tiny gold cables linked a miniature swatch of gold lamé fabric at her crotch to equally diminished coverings of her nipples. Nothing concealed her back at all, except for the loop of gold between her buttocks and around her neck. She wasn't artfully draped, merely artfully strung.

"Oh, my! This is outrageous!"

"I knew you'd like it." Dani pulled on his shorts and his polo shirt.

"I don't think I said that!"

"Hold still." He added a gold tiara and bracelets. Then he slipped some jeweled rings on her fingers.

Lori looked in the mirror. "What am I supposed to be?"

"Delicious!" he answered. Pulling on his shoes, he took her hand. "Ready?"

Lori smiled. "Why not?"

They went down to the party together.

2

I'll let your sister come along too

Naturally, all eyes went to Lori as they entered. The women seemed amused at her nerve, and the men were just agog. Conversation stopped.

Malcolm smiled and took her hands in greeting, wrapping his arms around her and pulling her close to him. "Thanks for taking the pressure off me. You must know I don't like being the center of attraction."

Lori kissed him and smiled. "I'm just looking forward to your announcement, Malcolm. Did I get dressed too quickly?"

He chuckled and continued holding her hand as he stepped back into the center of the room.

"Ladies and Gentlemen, I believe everyone is looking this way at the moment, so this may be the best opportunity to make my announcement."

"I have completed the mathematical analysis that will permit developing a sustained and controlled fusion reaction at a nominal cost. This fulfills the dream of Dr. Robert Bussard, whose visions of travel between planets and stars has illuminated the dreams and imaginations of researchers for hundreds of years."

"Prior to this time, the reactions in electrostatic confinement have been haphazard and fitful, barely achieving the break-even point, and quite insufficient for the kind of interstellar propulsion once envisioned."

"Thanks to a remarkable feedback system, a powerful reaction can now be sustained virtually indefinitely. My associates and I as of today have achieved a six month duration milestone of sustained fusion containment."

"Our first proposal is to mount the engine into a starcraft, and take a joyride around the solar system with it. We hope to be launching in six months."

Lori stepped away from him then, to join in the general applause. He scanned the room with a smile, and then he grabbed her hand again.

"I want you to go with us. Will you?"

"Really? Sure! But you'll have to bring my brother too. I won't go anywhere without him."

Malcolm looked a little disappointed. Lori thought she might have to make it up to him for that. But he brightened again immediately. It was, after all, his moment.

"He will be most welcome also." Malcolm looked around once more.

"Ladies and Gentlemen! As further demonstration of the feasibility of this innovation, I want you to witness with me the actual demonstration project. Our fusion engine has been keeping the lights on here for the last six months! Come and see it!"

Still holding Lori's hand, he escorted her and the others down two levels into a large helicopter hangar space. Dani followed along.

In the center of it, a brilliant light was blazing with a reddish-orange intensity. Surrounding it, racks and tiers of strange equipment rose to the high ceiling.

It would have been cold in the unheated space, but the abundant energy gave it a toasty warmth. Lori had presciently dressed quite appropriately.

Malcolm launched into a rapt description of the nature of his innovation, as Dani studied the rig. In addition to the standard arrangement of an ion trap surrounded by a soccer-ball lattice of electron clouds forming the virtual structure, all trapped within a magnetic spherical truss assembly, Malcolm had developed a non-physical wave-guide through carefully aligned microwave feeds.

Dani studied these. The equipment was monitoring all kinds of parameters of the whole reaction, but the interesting part was the microwave injection. Dani found the computer display that seemed to be isolating and controlling the pattern arrangement.

On six computer monitors, each showed an arrangement of polygon faces. Standing in front of this tableau was a tall man with long white hair.

Dani walked over to the man. "Professor Thornton?" Dani offered his hand.

The man turned. He smiled at Dani and shook hands with him.

"This monitors the injection array?" Dani asked.

Professor Thornton raised his white bushy eyebrows in surprise. "You're familiar with what we're doing here?"

"Call me Dani. You may remember my father. He went by the name of Blake Corrigan, a graduate student when you were lecturing at Columbia. I was an unofficial auditor of some of those classes a few years ago."

"I do recall seeing both of you! Blake was excellent, but you were there as well, big eyes and utter silence. I called you the ghost child. It's good to see you again!" He shook Dani's hand with a strong grip.

"You weren't at the party, Professor."

Thornton waved it away. "I'm a hundred and four. I don't have time for trifles." He turned back to the monitors.

Dani grew quiet as well. The display showed the faces of a three-dimensional structure that could only properly be visualized mentally. He called on his cybernetic associates to help him with the visualization.

After deducing the naming convention for the faces, he mentally assembled the structure with the information feed from the monitors. He frowned.

As elegant as the physical structure was, the synthetic wave-guide was a crude stick-like arrangement. Dani was aware that the magnetic latticework had suffered in the early days from being casually and manually constructed. He thought there might be a comparable way to improve the wave-guide function.

Obviously, the lattice end-points were the ones that needed the strength. If there were a way to change the alignment into a slight spiral, then the ribs of the virtual cage would be thinner, allowing a freer passage to the ionic flow. Dani went over the idea again, studying the way the injection manifolds were oriented.

"Professor Thornton, when the microwaves are injected, they travel exactly in alignment with the magnetic cage, don't they? Would it be possible to rotate the injection angle by five to ten degrees?"

Thornton looked at him. "That's the way we designed it, yes. We monitor it for exactly that alignment. You want to rotate the injection?" He looked distant and thoughtful for a few minutes. Then he sat down at the computer console and began poring over the control listing.

He halted at a particular point. "This is the alignment parameter. I'm going to introduce a new control. I'll put it right here on the computer keyboard. Every time I type R+ it will introduce a single degree of rotation into the matrix, on all injectors. Let's see what it does." He smiled at Dani.

He tapped the control and waited. Nothing happened. He tapped it three times more and waited again.

Still nothing.

Three more taps.

Was it his imagination, or was the sound of the background roar changing slightly, growing a little more deep-throated?

Three more taps. They waited.

Gradually, they became aware of a change. The light was growing brighter in color intensity, as if someone somewhere had slowly turned up the voltage.

Three more taps. Thirteen degrees of rotation.

Now they could see and hear the change in the chamber. The light was now distinctly more bluish in color, and the sound had grown into a deep-throated rumble like a powerful internal combustion engine.

Malcolm had stopped speaking and turned around, staring open-mouthed at the roaring blue fire.

Thornton studied another display. The output power had doubled.

He grinned at Dani in delight, and shook his hand excitedly. Malcolm saw them then, and stared at the old man and the boy.

Thornton stood up and clapped a hand on Dani's shoulder, smiling broadly at Malcolm with a devilish delight.

Staggering with the implications, Malcolm approached them. Lori followed behind him.

"What …?"

Thornton was still grinning. "Dani gave it a tune up. I'll put his name on my monograph."

Malcolm stared at him. Lori looked at him in astonishment.

Dani looked back with as mild an expression as he could muster. He had at last managed to impress his sister. He was very pleased.

Lori knelt down and gave him a big hug and kiss. "This is my brother, Dani." She looked back at Malcolm with tears in her eyes.

Attempting to recover his presence, Malcolm extended a hand. "By the way, I wanted to invite you to ride with us on our space venture. If you'd like, I'll let your sister come along too."

Dani grinned and shook hands. "Thanks, I'd like that. We'd both be honored."

Lori stood up and stared at Malcolm. He looked back mildly in unconscious repetition of Dani's deliberate acting of a moment ago.

Lori walked over and wrapped her arms around Malcolm, kissing him in an aggressive and predatory manner that bent his head back and buckled his knees.

If Malcolm had been staggering before, he was positively wobbly now as he walked back to the speaking area. Lori turned to Dani and said, "I'll probably be spending the night with him now. Will you be all right?"

Dani nodded. "I'll be fine."

Professor Thornton grasped for her hand and kissed it. "A pleasure to meet you, Miss Corrigan. Dani will be able to stay with me, if you don't mind. We may have things to discuss."

Dani and Lori looked at each other in surprise, but readily consented. Lori then left to pursue her wounded prey.

Professor Thornton introduced Dani to the rest of the current design and research team. He gave him access to their computer operations and a password so that he could work with them.

After several more hours of research analysis interrupted by partying, and of partying frequently interrupted by excited discussions about research analysis, Professor Thornton was ready to leave for some rest.

"I can show you where I live, Dani, and then you can come back here if you wish."

"That's all right, Professor. I'm ready to wind down myself. Let me walk with you."

"It isn't far. I have quarters on the lower level. Malcolm co-opted me a year ago."

They walked slowly to the professor's living quarters. More than half of the mountain house had been carved out of the rock of the mountain, and the corridors here were solid stone. The noise of the party and the fusion engine receded to silence.

Like the other parts of the house, the living room and the bedroom had a view window of the mountain scene. It also had about six thousand books, and several computer workstations and lab benches with various types of equipment.

"Ah, home at last." The Professor said. He approached a wet bar. "Name your poison. I need a drink."

"I don't drink, Professor. I'll have some soda water if you don't mind."

Thornton looked at him, seeming to notice once again that he appeared to be a child. He grew thoughtful.

"Columbia ... God, that was more than twenty years ago!" He stared at Dani and drank his drink, making a face. He looked up again. "How old are you?"

Dani spread his hands out in a modest gesture, an invitation to the professor to take a guess. Thornton snorted and mixed another drink.

Dani was looking around. Much of what he saw was completely unfathomable. Thornton smiled.

"You might like this." He rose from his chair and approached a raised platform. "It won't hurt you. Take your shoes off and stand up here."

Dani stood on the platform. He had no clue what its purpose was.

"Here. You'd better put this around your head, and cover your eyes." He held up a curious fabric, and nodded again, in reassurance.

Dani examined it. The material seemed to be some kind of woven ceramic. He put the wrap around his head in the manner of a turban.

It covered his head from the nape of his neck to the bridge of his nose. He stood quietly on the platform, waiting.

Professor Thornton could be heard rumbling around, making adjustments to his equipment, and then he threw a switch. "Hold still now." He called.

Dani could feel electrical discharges building up on his skin. It wasn't painful, but it tickled. He held still, not wanting to lose his balance.

Slowly a shrill whine built up, and he thought he might have been placed on a Van de Graaff generator. Odd crackling sounds emanated from his turban. Ionic winds blew about the surface of his skin.

Gradually, the whine dissipated and the tickling sensation went away. It was quiet again.

Professor Thornton said, "You can take off your cover now."

Dani unwrapped the fabric and looked down. A white powdery residue was on his skin. He was naked.

He looked around. The gray ash that remained of his clothing encircled the platform a couple of feet out. Not a trace of cloth or hair remained on his body where the wrap had not covered him.

Dani stepped down. His shoes were where he had left them. He put the ceramic fabric on one of the tables and looked at the professor.

Thornton had his head down on one hand while he tried not to spill his drink from laughter.

Dani smiled. He looked around and went into the bathroom to shower.

A few minutes later, he came back out again, still naked, but clean and dry. Utterly hairless, too, but he had been mostly that already. Lori would be pleased.

He sat on the couch, dangling his feet innocently.

Thornton was watching him. "You aren't mad, are you?"

Dani shook his head. "That's a neat device. It didn't hurt at all."

Thornton sipped his drink. They watched each other for a while.

Dani got up and wandered around the room, looking at the various devices and mechanisms. From time to time he looked back to see what the professor was doing, only to see Thornton glancing away. Being stared at naked bothered Dani no more than it did Lori.

Presently, Dani found a way to play some music. He selected a special score and turned up the volume.

Then he danced.

He and Lori had taken dance lessons together, and they could still perform some of the routines. This would have to be a solo act, however. That wasn't a problem, because this particular selection was one that cried out for joyous, exuberant expression.

Dani skipped across the floor in a happy imitation of Olympic free-style floor gymnastics, leaping and twirling, and emoting for all he was worth.

He was having fun. It had been some time since he had given free expression to his joy.

He caught a glimpse of his observer. Professor Thornton was weeping, and he had closed his eyes.

Dani went to him and held his hands. Thornton opened his eyes.

"Thank you." The old man said.

Dani sat beside him and laid his head on Thornton's knee. Gradually a wrinkled old hand came to rest gently on his shoulder. The old man slowly swept his hand down along Dani's flank to his hip and his rump, and then brought it up once more.

Again and again, he petted Dani like a cat or dog. Dani lay still.

Professor Thornton sighed.

"Oh, Dani, what are you?"

Dani sat up and held the old man's hand. "A friend," he said.

"Go and take your shower now, Professor. You are going to need your rest."

Thornton sighed again and slowly stood up. "There are bedclothes in those drawers over there. You can make up the couch to sleep on." He looked down sadly at Dani. "You're right. It's been a long day." He slowly ambled away into the bathroom.

Dani listened as the old man went through his routine. He heard him get into bed and lie still, sighing once more in the stillness.

Then Dani arose and got in the bed with him, snuggling close to him as if for warmth.

3

How do you bend the rays?

(Tuesday, May 27, 2142)
Timeline: _____|_____

The next morning, Dani was awakened by the touch of a hand alongside his cheek. Professor Thornton had already risen and dressed. He was sitting at an angle to the bed and watching Dani. He looked either depressed or very determined.

"Tell them I'll be in about … Tell them I'll be in later. You go and help them with today's adjustments. I need to take care of some personal business."

"Are you okay, Professor?"

"I'm … better. I *will* be okay. Thank you, Dani." He leaned down to kiss Dani and then quickly departed, walking with an erect posture that belied his many years.

Dani watched him out of sight and then stretched languidly. Presently he got up.

As Dani was tidying up about the apartment, he spotted a discarded lab smock. He put it on. It was ludicrously oversized for him. He liked it.

The sleeves were too long, so he cut them off. Then he wrapped the garment over itself and secured the loose end with a clasp from the desk. The shirt pocket of the smock was centered on his chest like the pocket of a bib overall.

He put some clip pens and a pocket thermosensor in the pocket and looked in the mirror.

Ah, one more touch was needed. He put on his sneakers again.

Perfect. A nerd warrior ready to venture forth and do battle. Dani went back up to the hangar deck.

The experiment was still running, and still burning with the blue intensity. Three other researchers were there, but only one recognized him as the one who had suggested the innovation that had doubled their efficiency.

Dani relayed to them that Professor Thornton was away on personal business.

Charlie explained to the others, Wade and Richard, that Dani and Thornton had worked together on the modifications. He was still puzzled, though.

"I thought last night that I understood what happened, but I've been studying it this morning and I don't see why the changes you made had such a difference. I can't even imagine how you knew to do it."

"I'm not sure I can tell you precisely, but I might be able to show you. Do we have a holographic projector?"

"We can get one." Wade responded.

Soon they had the new equipment installed and synchronized. Dani called up a simulation of their experiment, and then stripped away the physical, and the fusor operations. He was displaying only the microwave wave-guide function, but this time in three dimensions.

"This was what I saw. Look it over."

Richard said, "That's the way we set it up. We've established a wave sheath that protects the hardware, and keeps the ion temperature up. What's wrong with it?"

"Look at the ion path into the chamber. Wait a minute. I'll change to a strobe between the original set-up and our modification. Do you see it now?"

"I'm seeing something. It looks like the linear portions are getting thinner. How do you do that? I don't know how to bend electromagnetic radiation in a vacuum."

"Let's try this: Reverse image, a negative. These are the ionic openings into the chamber. It's still on a half-second strobe."

"Oh, I see it now. It's like an hourglass, and you've made the opening larger. Naturally you get a faster flow rate."

"And it doesn't change the basic configuration. It just increases the collision rate."

"Right. But back to the previous question, how do you bend the rays?"

"That's what I saw. I was picturing this image in my mind, and I saw that these bars are not solid at all, even in their geometry. They are like a ring of soda straws wrapped around a dowel. They would assume the shape of the dowel."

Heads nodded.

Dani continued. "But this isn't physical. If you remove the dowel, the soda straw column is still columnar, of course. Now, imagine holding each end, and giving it a slight twist. The tube of columnar straws will pinch in the middle, while remaining the same dimension at each end."

Dani isolated a single element, and showed how the slight rotation pinched the center slightly.

Wade's eyes were practically glowing. "I see it! Ingenious! But what about circularly polarizing the injected wave, and letting it wrap around on the way to the next junction? We could make it even tighter, which means we could run the same power in a half-sized fusor!"

"Or even resuscitate the egg configuration! Remember, we couldn't establish a stable ion trap in that before, but I think we can with this technique."

At this time, Lori appeared. As was not uncommon for her, the conversation stopped abruptly.

She was wearing yet another new outfit. A shimmering green ribbon wound its way around her body like a spiral groove, from her neck down to just above her knees. It was almost a dress.

Her nipples peeked impertinently out from between the bands of ribbon. How she kept everything in alignment could not be discerned.

She looked at Dani in disappointment. "Oh, no. That won't do at all. Come along, brother. Let me get you dressed so that you can meet someone." She reached for his left hand.

Dani looked around. "Sorry, fellows. Duty calls. I guess we can play later."

"You go ahead, Dani. We've got the idea now. We can take it from here for a while." Charlie said. All three shook hands with him before he left.

Dani walked with his sister. "Nice outfit!"

"Thanks. What the heck are you supposed to be, a coat-rack?"

"You don't like it?" Dani emptied his pocket contents onto a table. He didn't think the rest of his costume would last much longer. He thought of disintegrating it for her.

"We're going to meet someone today. Malcolm's sponsor, the person who developed this facility and lured these people here. Now, how shall we make you presentable to Miss Alicia?" She took him to bedroom eleven B.

Dani accepted her leadership. Socially, she was more comfortable with people than he was, and more tuned in to their sensitivities. Maybe he just liked being mothered.

"All right, go get cleaned up. I'll order an outfit for you, as soon as I think of something. And I'll get rid of these rags."

Dani grinned and got out of his nerd suit. He took a shower.

When he saw the costume she had selected, he almost burst into laughter. A white frilled shirt with puffy sleeves, short black pants, and dark shoes. He would look like Little Lord Fauntleroy!

Dani hoped that this Miss Alicia would appreciate the indignities he was about to undergo for her sake.

He got dressed, feeling very much the young dandy. At least he wouldn't have to defend his honor in a schoolyard.

Lori smiled. "Now, that's much better. Let's find Malcolm."

As they walked, Dani tried to feel uncomfortable, but he didn't. In general, he liked wearing shorts. These pants, while a little snug, were flexible and easy to move in. The shirt was airy and silken. He looked the dandy, but he felt comfortable. Maybe he could accessorize with a rapier. He smiled.

Lori smiled back at him. "That's the spirit! We want to make a good impression."

Dani was left to figure out why it was important that they made a good impression. He couldn't think of a reason he might want to.

Then he saw Miss Alicia.

She had Lori's beauty, with a calm, assured demeanor indicating she was used to being in charge, and being respected. While Lori's clothing style represented modern expressions, hers indicated a more refined dignity. Almost lost in the spectacle of her presence was the young lady at her side, a girl of the apparent age of twelve or thirteen. She seemed to be only an inch or two above Dani's height.

When he was presented, Dani made a courtly bow.

"Dani, is it? Well, young man, you seem to have impressed my associates here, and after only an evening. May I present my niece Anastasia? You two may share an interest in music, from what I hear."

Dani kissed Anastasia's hand. Might as well go for the whole effect.

Presently the talk devolved to minor details about Malcolm's intended launch date, and the funding and site preparation work still needed. Dani found himself shuttled aside with Anastasia.

"Would you care for some refreshment, Miss Anastasia?" he asked.

"Please! And call me Ana, if you don't mind, Danny."

He lightly corrected her pronunciation, spelling his name out for her. It was more a matter of equal emphasis on the two syllables than the typically heavy accentuation of Dan in Danny. He wasn't picky, but it helped people to remember how to spell it.

Dani fetched some fruit punch for them, and suggested a small divan in the corner where they could sit.

Ana seemed pleased.

"We've been traveling most of the morning. This is our third business meeting today. We'll probably have two more."

"You have my sympathies. Maybe you could bail out and just hang around here."

"And do what?"

34

"Nothing. Same as me. What would you like to do?" They sat down on the little couch.

"I'd like to stay and swim. That would be refreshing, and restful. Have you seen the pool here?"

"I haven't seen it yet. I love swimming. It gives me the chance to ogle the chicks."

She smiled. "You're dressed very nicely for someone so outspoken, Dani."

He looked down, holding out his arms. "My sister's idea. I like her designs for herself, but she has some weird ideas for how to dress me. This morning, she wanted me to play Cupid, with my bare butt hanging out."

Ana sipped her punch. "You have my sympathies in return. This is my Aunt's idea."

Dani raised his glass. "We are prisoners of our relatives."

"Aunt Alicia said that you were an accomplished musician."

"I sat in with a group here last night. Stringed instruments. Nimble fingers and no need for a lot of wind power."

"You're very modest."

Dani smiled and looked away.

"Would you really have worn a Cupid costume? With your bare butt hanging out?"

He looked at her with an impish grin. "Absolutely! I like having fun, too."

"That might have been interesting to see."

Dani looked in her eyes. "How do you swim?"

Her face reddened. "Perhaps I was wrong about your being modest!"

Dani smiled. "I have lots I can be modest about. Skin isn't something that bothers me. With a sister like mine, you get over that sort of thing."

"She's very beautiful."

"So is your aunt, and so are you."

"You really think so? With two gorgeous women in the room, you think *I'm* beautiful?"

"Yes. I'd like to see you in your bathing suit, or however you swim."

"Oh, you *are* smooth!"

Dani smiled again. "We could play music instead. I have some violin favorites you might enjoy. Do you play?"

"Keyboardist."

"Excellent! Piano and violin go well together."

Ana got up and went over to speak with her aunt. After several minutes, she returned.

"I'm staying."

"I'm tempted to kiss you. I'd better behave myself. Would you like more punch?"

"We'll get around to it. Yes, please."

When Dani returned, Ana's aunt was speaking quietly to her. Dani held back until they finished.

"Thank you again." Ana accepted the punch.

"Any other ideas? I've only been here for about a day. I haven't seen much, except the fusion lab, and Professor Thornton's apartment."

Ana looked at him curiously. "You were in Professor Thornton's quarters? Are you, um … are you feeling okay?"

"Sure! He was looking at me, if that's what you mean. I danced for him. I don't think he would have lost control if I had begged him to. He seemed a little sad."

Ana digested this slowly. "You danced for him?"

Dani nodded. "I've studied ballet."

"Ballet too? What haven't you studied?"

"I haven't studied Russian, yet. Never had occasion to visit there."

"Вам повезет!" Ana said.

Dani tilted his head for a moment. "Я не изучал русский, однако, Ana."

"How did you do that?"

"My parents didn't want to waste money for a college education on me, so they stuffed a computer in my head."

"Amazing! What other secrets do you have?"

Dani took her cup from her and set it aside. "If I told you, they wouldn't be secrets anymore. May we walk?"

"My pleasure, Sir!"

They went down to the hangar deck, and observed the ongoing

fusion program. Wade was the first to see him. He rolled his eyes in mock horror and shook his head. The others waved.

Dani and Ana waved back.

"Aunt Alicia said that you had something to do with the jump in efficiency. Did you?"

Dani nodded. "That's how I caught the eye of the Professor. I may be his new protégé."

Ana looked dubious. "Where is the Professor, anyway? He's usually here."

"He left this morning on a personal errand. He asked me to tell them he would be in later."

Ana had been looking around. She rotated back to looking at Dani with an exaggeratedly slow turn. "Are you saying that you *spent the night* with him?" She whispered.

Dani faced her calmly. "He was a perfect gentleman. So was I, for that matter. Except for the dancing, maybe."

She stared at him. "You are messing with my head. *How old are you?*"

Dani turned her, and began walking out into the corridor. "I think that would be one of those secrets I mentioned."

"I can find out. I have resources too. Please! I just want to understand. It could even be important. Tell me how old you are, please."

They stopped at a spot in the corridor where a bench seat offered a view through yet another simulated window. Dani sat down with her.

"All right, … I was born in the last century. My father got me a genetic preservation treatment when I was ten years old. My sister Lori is my *younger* sister, by more than twenty years."

"I *knew* it!" Ana smiled at him. "I have a secret to confess as well. … My "Aunt Alicia" is actually my *daughter!* I let her act as my business manager, while I occupy myself with more interesting pursuits."

"Whoa! That changes things!"

"It certainly does. Tell me something else, then. If you really didn't have sex with Professor Thornton, *why* didn't you?"

Dani related the whole incident, from the vaporization of his clothes to the suggestion that he make up a pallet on the couch, and his subsequent getting into bed with the old man anyway.

Ana was nodding her head. "Yeah. That holds together. You know what? I think the reason the Professor didn't put more of a move on you was because he came to love you too much."

"That sounds right."

"Where do you think he went?"

Dani shrugged. "No idea. He seemed determined about something. Or depressed. That's all I can say."

Ana looked around. "Let's go this way." She led him further along the corridor, and then down a side corridor. This place was enormous!

They entered the swimming pool. It was dark, with exotic plants growing around the walls, and soft music playing. The pool was lit from underneath, glowing a blue and shimmering invitation.

Without a word, Ana took off her clothes and waited.

Dani removed his shoes, shirt and pants, and stacked them neatly on a chair. He turned to look at the girl.

She had a trim waist, with very small hips, and just barely swelling breasts. Her slim body seemed just on the verge of pubescence.

Ana looked with equal frankness at his body, seeing a thin but healthy boy, with curly brown hair and no sign at all of pubic awakening. His features were, in a word, cherubic.

"Do you have sex at all?" She asked him.

"Yes. Most recently I spent a very enjoyable evening with my sister."

"Your sister?"

"We've had a lot of practice."

Ana tilted her head quizzically.

"I don't usually try to take advantage of kids, even though I get a lot of opportunities. I've learned that restraint can be as entertaining and fun as debauchery might. Just being with someone, lying next to them, is more than enough to satisfy me. It's easy to keep my sex drive at low idle."

"Would you like to have sex with me?"

"Very much so. Are you in a hurry?"

"No. No hurry at all." Ana stepped forward and embraced him, pulling him into a shared warmth. They kissed.

After a moment, they walked over to the pool edge and sat with their feet in the water. Dani kicked his feet and watched the ripples spread across the pool.

"How do you manage that?" Ana asked, pointing at his crotch.

"It isn't difficult. I have complete control over it. One of the things that guys can be embarrassed about is an uncontrolled reaction. That's why most of them are self-conscious about being naked in company. It doesn't bother me because I never have an erection unless I want to. Like the rest of me, it's a little small."

He shrugged. "I guess you know that partners can be flexible about that. More importantly from that standpoint, I can also control how long I sustain my erection. My sex partners have never complained."

"I think I'm in love."

Dani laughed. Ana joined him.

Behind them, the door opened. Lori entered, having changed to a simple tennis dress. She took her shoes off and sat beside Dani.

"You two seem to be getting along well." She said.

"We were just talking about when we are going to have sex." Dani responded.

Lori looked over at Ana. "You'll find that he talks about that a lot."

Ana replied coolly, "Dani said that his sex partners have never complained."

"As far as I know, that's true. I certainly never have."

"So you really do! Brother and sister, I mean? That's wonderful!"

"Yes it is." Lori responded, "Nobody pleases me better."

From his sitting position, Dani bowed.

"I suppose I should leave then." Lori said.

"Only if you want to. All we've done so far is kiss. She hasn't even gotten around to kicking the tires yet."

"Dani is a sweet kisser." Lori said to Ana.

"I have noticed that, but I need some more samples to be sure. Would you care to stay? We really are only talking so far."

"Perhaps another time. It would be very entertaining to observe. But I have agreed to play tennis with someone. There are indoor tennis courts down in the village. You two have fun!"

"You do the same!" Ana replied.

Dani stood up when Lori did, and kissed her goodbye. She placed her hand on his buttock and squeezed it gently as they kissed, and then winked at Ana. "*Very* sweet kisses!" She said.

They watched her leave. Dani sat down again.

"She really is quite fond of you. You're very lucky."

Dani nodded. "I've cultivated that friendship for quite a while. When she was a little girl, I changed my sexual identity so that we could be sisters together. I think it meant a lot to her."

"You changed to being a girl? I didn't know that was possible! Or that anyone would be willing to do it. You really are amazing!"

"I can't do it at the drop of a hat. I don't have *that* much control. The process took about three months, going both ways. I maintained the gender switch for fourteen years while she was growing up. For a time, we were exactly the same size, and we dressed as twins. It was a lot of fun."

"Aw! You must love her very much!"

"I do. I find it easy to love people. Most of them treat me with great kindness, although many of them are rather dismissive of me. That doesn't bother me as much as you might think, because it tells me *volumes* about those types."

"I know *exactly* what you mean! Oh, what a treasure you are! I think I've found my long-lost brother." She leaned her head against his shoulder.

Dani tilted her face up and kissed her again. "That's a good thing. You know how I feel about sisters."

Ana smiled.

4

I think I'm in love

Ana's living quarters were the most posh in the residence. The finest fabrics, artworks, and accessories were on display.

Dani was on display as well.

"Dance for me," She had said, "the way you did for Thorny."

This time, he was better prepared. Selecting a recording of the '27 version of the stage play, "Pan Triumphant", he improvised the scene of Pan rising like Venus, in an arboreal glade. His slow, weaving motions, like a plant seeking the light, gradually changed to a merry dance of joy for the awakening morning, and for life.

After about twenty minutes of quite vigorous exercise, as the music crescendoed and then quieted, Dani ended the dance with raised hands. He was in this pose when "Aunt Alicia" entered the apartment. Dani bowed, to Ana's applause, then he dropped to his knees for a rest.

Alicia approached the two of them with an unreadable expression. Ana looked up mildly.

"Would you care to explain yourself?" Alicia looked sternly at her.

"Certainly. I have found the most amazingly compliant and cooperative young man. He does everything I tell him to do. Dani, come here please."

Dani got up nimbly and presented himself to the two women. He stood naked and unconcerned, and inwardly amused. He smiled.

"Anastasia! What do you think you're doing?" Alicia stood with her fists on her hips, the very picture of outrage.

"I'm amusing myself. I think I'll stay here for a few weeks having fun. I won't be needing anything."

Alicia looked in astonishment at Dani.

He shrugged. "Your mother probably needs a break from her busy schedule."

Now Alicia's jaw dropped. "You *told* him?" She stared at Ana.

Ana nodded. "It is the oddest thing. That beautiful girl downstairs that we met today? Lori Corrigan?" Ana looked at Dani. "Lori is Dani's *younger* sister."

Now a panoply of emotions crossed Alicia's face, finally ending in bewilderment.

"Oh!"

"Dani is actually older than I am. We're going to shack up together for a while and have rapturous, glorious sex, while you go out and make more money to support us."

Dani approached the confused young lady and helped her to a seat. She looked into his eyes in wonder.

"Is this true?"

He nodded. Then he turned in place, letting her see his glorious, rapturous boy body.

"I don't know how many like us there are, but it is difficult for us to find each other. One thing that makes the quest worthwhile is that we can afford to be patient." He smiled.

"Mother … Oh, my, that is so strange! I so seldom get a chance to use the word. It seems I play the role of responsible adult so much I tend to let it go to my head. Mother, will you be all right here?"

"Oh, yes dear. Dani and I have a lifetime to catch up on. We'll have fun here, and if we get bored, we'll go pester the geniuses downstairs."

"You'll be able to get in touch with me if you need anything. Do be careful! I'll miss you." The reversed role mother and daughter hugged each other. Then Alicia embraced Dani as well.

"Kiss him too." Ana said.

Alicia kissed Dani.

"Well? What do you think? Is he sweet?"

Alicia looked at Dani, and kissed him again, longer this time.

"Oh, yes, mother. He is adorably sweet."

"He followed me home. Can I keep him?" Ana asked in a childlike voice.

Alicia smiled. "Funny, I was going to ask you the same thing." She put her hands up on Dani's shoulders, feeling the structure of them as she looked again with new understanding at his pre-pubescent body. "How do they do it, Dani? You look like a boy, not a small man."

"My father is now sixty-seven years old. He looks like a man in his forties. My mother is sixty-three, and she looks like a woman in her thirties. We all underwent the same process, which gives our nanobots a framework and blueprint to follow to keep us the way we were thirty years ago. On them it looks nice. On me, it looks a little weird. I was ten when I got blueprinted."

"Do you have regrets?"

Dani smiled. "No. I loved life when I was ten years old, and I have loved every day of my life since then. I don't know if the "blueprinting" carries forward to the extent that what I liked to do then some nanobot is telling me I'll enjoy today, but whatever the reason is, I do still enjoy it. I love playing sports, swimming, bicycle riding, and all of those boy things. But I also love reading books, playing and listening to music, quiet walks, moonlight, rainbows, sunsets and sunrises, scientific research and new technology, pretty girls and pretty women, and having all the time in the world to enjoy them."

Ana applauded. "I think you're going to be good for me!"

Alicia sighed. "All right, you two. Have fun. I'll go out and be responsible." She kissed Dani one more time, hugged and kissed her mother, and departed the room, stopping once to look back at them and to shake her head in amazement.

"You dance well." Ana said.

"Thank you. I love dancing."

"Dance with me!" Ana said abruptly, and then softened, "Please?"

He took her hand as she rose and held her. This close together, with her fully clothed and him naked, the disparity of their sizes was apparent. He was looking up at her eyes.

They danced, slowly, holding each other in a long, twirling hug.

Ana stopped, and held him still. She kissed him, for a long moment.

"I'd like to take you to bed now, Dani."

Dani smiled. "I'm ready."

5

Do you have regrets?

"He was young, then. Just sixteen. Now he's balding and paunchy. I keep tabs on him, but we don't have anything to do with him. If he had stood by us when we needed him, it would be a different story."

"I'm sorry."

"It's for the best, I'm sure. If he couldn't face his responsibilities then, he certainly would not have dealt well with our "unique" situation."

"Yeah. Things got a little confusing and stressful for us as well. I think Dad took it hardest. Mom got everything she secretly wanted, but Dad lost out on a son to follow in his footsteps. I don't think I realized just how my cross-gender masquerade chewed at him at the time."

"Tell me about it."

"It was my idea. We were keeping our special circumstances secret at the time. You never know how people will react to such things. We had trouble getting nannies and baby-sitters, and I thought it was wasteful to even bother."

"When Lori was born, I was twenty-four. I thought I could care for her as well as anyone else. Mother suggested that it just wouldn't pass neighborhood scrutiny for Lori to be in the charge of a young boy. So I piped up that I would just become a girl for a while."

"At first, Mother didn't think I was serious, or that it could even be done. Then I talked to Dad about it too. I needed his help anyway."

"He was surprisingly cooperative, considering. He explained that my nanobots would have to be temporarily modified. Rather than change their program entirely, they simply put a time-function into it. Nanobots have their own time, but they also have a gene clock they can access. There are counters that don't seem to feed into control systems. Some researchers speculate that they inform instinct algorithms. Humans tend not to rely on instincts, but the programming is still there.

"Anyway, the rewrite was only intended to be effective for a set length of time. It turned out to be about fourteen years. During that time, my Y chromosome template was de-emphasized, and my X chromosome instructions were given priority. It worked well enough.

"There are sufficient examples of genetic males who have female anatomy, that the genes involved have been identified. It only required a small number of control resets. Slowly my anatomy changed, as my external bits receded and the skin turned inside out.

"My gonads pulled up inside the abdomen again, and in just a few months, I was anatomically a girl. I had to be especially careful about peeing, and staying very clean, but because my body was still at a stage where boys and girls resemble each other a lot, no other modifications were needed.

"Dad went on to adapt the system to being able to initiate the firewall without freezing young people in pre-adolescence. Parents could get the protection they wanted, but the child could still grow up.

"I think that discovery helped Dad a lot in his career. I'm sure he felt better about himself after that, too."

Ana was leaning on her side with one hand supporting her head. Her other hand idly traced along Dani's skin as he reminisced. He lay still and spoke softly.

"What was it like, becoming a girl?" Ana asked.

"There were a lot of rules I had to remember. I wore dresses for the first time. Not that I was really looking forward to it. But it was part of the masquerade, so I had to do it."

"Mother loved it. She saw it as a precursor to having Lori to dress up. Actually, she had both of us to dress up, and she did it with delight. The especially frilly dresses and fancy outfits were a bit of a pain, because I had to keep them clean and all. And then Mother insisted that I grow my hair long as well. It's a bit naturally curly, so she would put it up into ringlets and other girly styles. Sometimes when I saw myself in the mirror, I didn't recognize myself!"

"But the thing that made it worthwhile was that we didn't need to have a babysitter or nanny. I was able to care for Lori myself, when Mother wasn't around, and it was great fun for both of us."

"We shared everything in those days. We slept in the same bed, bathed together, dressed in similar outfits, and went to parties together."

"And to make it even better, Lori was growing up! When she got to be nearly my size, we started pretending to be twins. That was fun! We did everything together."

"And of course, by then we had started having fun with each other's bodies. We both learned a lot."

"How old were you then?"

"Lori was close to ten, so I was about thirty. You might think I was a grown man, but I hadn't grown, remember? I did kid things in those days, because that's what I was involved with being. You've seen kids who act mature and serious, and some adults can be silly when they want to, but I was just being natural. It took me a long time to realize that if I was ever going to do anything *other than* be a kid, I would have to do it by sheer mental effort. My body wanted me to do kid things. It's still that way today."

"Lori kept growing, and getting more beautiful all the time. Pretty soon I was just her kid sister. We couldn't be twins anymore. We grew a little apart then, but we still stayed in the same room, and slept together. We enjoyed the growth of her breasts together."

"Having Lori help me with my makeup was more fun than having Mom do it. I practiced being and acting feminine, partly for Lori's sake. We had the ballet lessons and things like a charm school that Mother found. When I want to be, I can act the perfect lady, or gentleman."

"I've noticed that. You do have exemplary manners."

"It pays. People treat you better when you act as though you think they should. It actually makes it more comfortable for them as well."

"And then you changed back?"

"Yes. Lori was eighteen. I changed back into a boy. We didn't make it a big deal, but we continued sleeping together. By then, I had worked out some of the details about how I could modify myself. It was always a possibility for me to have an erection. When I was a boy, that is. But I found the triggers that let me control it consciously, and I also had a path to other parameters that I could access. Erection size isn't correlated with bone length, as you may be aware."

"It seems strange, but even with this as a starting point, I can get considerable size increase, and still go back to the inoffensive size that I had before."

"Yes, I'm aware of that."

"Oh, yes. Right. Where was I?"

"You were talking about producing a large erection."

"I was? Are you sure about that?"

"Oh yes. It was definitely a consideration." Ana was moving her hand up and down his smooth skin as she spoke. (Tue 27 May 2142)

6

What was it like?

"Mr. Blake Corrigan?"

"Yes, Doctor Thornton. It's good to see you again. You're looking well."

"Considering, you mean to say. You don't look a day older, yourself."

"Thank you."

"It isn't a compliment. It's an observation. I've recently seen your son. He also appears to be not a day older. On him, that is a more impressive accomplishment."

"Please sit down, Doctor Thornton. I'm curious why you requested this clandestine meeting."

"Thank you. I have sought you out because I may need your help and advice."

"I would be absolutely thrilled to be able to help you, Professor. But I hope I don't have to be the bearer of bad tidings. To be quite frank, we are not the kind of miracle workers that some rumors have alleged."

"I am familiar with some of the limitations. To be equally honest, it was seeing your son that confirmed my decision."

"How so?"

"Many years ago, I approached some people about the possibility of doing something to protect and extend my health. I went through a battery of tests, and eventually ended with a very basic form of protection. My concern at the time was that I wanted to be assured that any procedure would not prevent me from developing advanced mental concepts."

"To my regret, they were unable to assuage my concerns. I am familiar with such things as the early stages of Alzheimer's and other forms of dementia. One of the significant observations is that humans have a wealth of coping strategies, by which they continue to seem utterly normal. Presumably, there's nothing wrong with being normal, but I work in a field of exceptional people."

"I remember." Blake responded.

Thornton nodded, and continued. "Then I met Dani. If my concern had any merit, Dani would have been the exemplar of a person in frozen mental development. He was not."

"I do hope you're going to explain that." Blake smiled encouragingly.

Professor Thornton paused, and chuckled. "Yes, I suppose you would be interested. For the past year, I have been working in a development project involving advanced concepts in fusion reactions. We were very proud of our accomplishments, and had held a public presentation to display the results. Your son showed up, and in fifteen minutes, discovered something that had eluded us from the beginning. His vision gave us the capability of doubling our efficiency, and may lead to further refinements in capabilities. I concluded that his mental functioning was not impaired in any way."

"I ... see. Thank you for sharing that with me."

"There's more. I was also impressed with Dani's ... let's call it social maturity. His deceptively youthful appearance masks not only a bright mind, but a patient and tolerant attitude as well. By the way, how old is he really?"

Blake considered. "Dani is forty-three. God! How I wish I could drink when I say that!"

"What do you mean?"

"One of the side effects of the process we use. Among other things, alcohol is an energy source for the nanobots. While they may be having a high old time, for me, the alcohol is just another flavor."

"Dani said he didn't drink. Maybe I should have done more research."

Blake sat quietly for a moment. "So you've changed your mind about something. What is it you think I can help you with?"

"I suppose I've come to the realization that I should have used that process about thirty years ago, when I was thinking about it. I'd like to know if there is anything that can be done now."

Blake drummed his fingertips. "It depends. Do you know what level of analysis was used?"

"Not really. It seemed extensive. Here are the details as far as I could reconstruct them."

"Oh, that's great! I'll follow up on what information may still be available. This could literally be a life-saver."

"Well, I'm in the position of needing that. I'm now a hundred and four."

Blake blinked. It was hard not to be astonished. "You're doing very well on your own."

"We both know that won't last much longer."

"With luck, the records will be complete enough that we could restore you to the apparent age you were then."

"Hmph. I had hoped, and feared, that you might say that. Another reason I approached you in particular. That simply won't be good enough. I want to be taken back to Dani's apparent age."

Blake got up and went to the room's wet bar. Using unspoken signals only, he mixed drinks for both of them.

"It's extraordinarily dangerous to try to mix genomic information in this way. Human beings sort this kind of thing out in the womb. The fatal combinations simply disappear. We can't even calculate the odds. I've read papers that detail some of the things that can go wrong. One of the more prosaic is that your entire personality could be subsumed by the intruding data swarm."

Thornton sipped his drink calmly. "I'm aware of that. I consider it an acceptable risk."

Blake looked intensely at him. "There are other risks as well. Ones so dire that the company has already issued instructions against such activities. I could set this up as an investigatory possibility, but any actual attempt would have to be done under complete secrecy. Not only my career and fortune, but your legal existence, would be threatened."

"I understand. It's clear that I came to the right person. At least you're willing to consider it, despite its being illegal and against company policy."

"I've always been rather cautious at work. This is a bit out of character for me. It's possibly for that reason that I might be able to get away with it." He looked thoughtful.

"Do you have any idea how much it will cost?"

Blake looked intently at him once more. "That much I do know. It will cost you everything you have."

Again Thornton sipped his drink with exaggerated calm. "I had suspected as much. That seems fair."

"The only possibility is that you surrender all your worldly assets to the company, and then disappear as a legal entity. You will legally at least become a different person. If we are successful in changing your appearance as you hope, you may have to be adopted by someone. I wouldn't mind, but it can't be me."

"I understand. What can you tell me about the process, if you think there is a faint possibility?"

"We'll marry the nanobot information together. As far as we are able, we'll check for incompatible insertions, deletions, reversals, and heaven knows what other kinds of potential problems. Then we'll build a template using Dani's blueprint as a pattern to follow. Damn, this is dangerous! It's also a bit thrilling to contemplate. One of the reasons we gravitated to this kind of research in the first place."

"It will be an all or nothing situation. Once the instruction set is completed, that's going to become the new you, for better or worse. Possibly, there's only a one in twelve chance that you will survive. You could die in the first three days. But anyway, after we introduce the nanobots into you, there is absolutely no going back. We have to get it right the first time, because we can't un-colonize you. It would be like trying to round up all the rabbits in Australia."

"Assuming it works, how long would it take?"

"Four or five months. If it goes perfectly, you will shed weight like a dying man. I have no idea if there will be pain or discomfort; I expect there will be. During the process, you will probably look distorted, even hideous. Doctor Thornton, could anything at all be worth this risk?"

Thornton smiled. "Yes. Life could be worth it. Trust me; I would not be risking much, or losing much."

"I'll see what I can do. God help me! I always knew I could turn into Victor Frankenstein, if I haven't already."

"You've done some remarkable work. I have confidence."

"I wish I did. We'll be getting in touch with you. Good Luck!"

"Good Luck to you as well."

"Thanks! Man, I wish I could drink!"

"In sympathy, I might try giving it up myself." Professor Thornton smiled as he made his way to the door.

* * *

"How's it going, Fellows?" Blake stuck his head into the imaging theater.

"Have a look." Rob Jennison responded. "We've set up two tracks, labeled DC1 to DC2, and ET1 to ET2. D is superposed above T. We've established one to one links for more than ninety-eight percent of the paired genomes, with some interesting observations."

Blake studied the floating images for a while. What he was observing looked like a railroad yard switching system. Lines of color-coded transcriptions floated in the vast chamber.

"What's this notation? I don't remember it."

Rob grinned. "It's a shame you don't recognize your own handiwork. That's a denotation of the genomic clock. Both of these depictions show a time-separation of about thirty years. Thirty years! I was just a kid! Here's the interesting thing; when you compare to the telomere markers, there's a big discrepancy. And that's not all. We think we've found three more marking systems. Comparing these two genetic tracks is giving us a lot of information, primarily because they are time-synched. We're seeing what happens as an individual genome ages."

"What about inversions and deletions?"

"Some very small areas. We don't think they are functional. Greg thinks we can push a model through right away. I'm not so sure. I'd like to identify the tertiary and quaternary markers before we do the build."

"Win, lose or draw, we're going to have to wrap up this phase in two weeks. That's the limit for analysis. Trying to stretch it any further will put a red flag on it."

"That will be risky. It's like asking a surgeon to work in the dark. I hope this patient isn't a member of your family."

"I'm hoping it won't be that bad. Let's see what we can do with what we have."

* * *

7

If my concern had any merit

"Here's what we've come up with, Doc." Blake began immediately. "Of the six researchers privy to the truth, all have concluded that the process will likely be fatal. The problem is the number of unknowns. We don't know how your body will react to the introduction of the nanobots. You could easily die of fever. We don't know whether the nanobots will be able to identify and preserve enough of your tissues to keep you alive as the changes are implemented."

"Accordingly, we've worked out a scenario, using the minimum number of nanobots, to reduce the possibility of overreaction, either of your natural defenses or the rapidity of the conversion process. This will stretch out the timeline. If it happens to be uncomfortable, it will be uncomfortable for a very long time. That's the best we can do."

"Assuming everything works perfectly, and I survive the process, what is the resultant appearance that I could expect, and how long would it take?" Thornton replied calmly.

"If it works, you'll be reduced in stature, your skin and hair will be regenerated, and you'd weigh about half what you do now. It would take about a hundred days. Your exact appearance, we can't predict."

"It's your best shot?"

Blake nodded. "As much as possible, we did a one-to-one correspondence between your reverse-extrapolated genome, and that of my own son's beginning record. What we can't predict is how you will fare during the transition."

Thornton nodded. "You've prepared the potion?"

Blake looked down. "It's ready. We're recommending against it, you know?"

"I know. It could kill me. You realize that I would likely be dead in another year anyway?"

"I understand why you think it may be worth the risk, but you may not entirely appreciate how distressful it could be."

"True. But I do appreciate your concern, and that of the others. Let's do it anyway."

Blake sighed. "I knew it would come to this. You're aware that we will have to concoct a plausible death for you, even if you survive? We'll need to protect the company's interests."

"That will be no concern of mine. One way or another, this life is now over."

"And you realize that the easy thing for us to do would be to simply poison you and eliminate the problem?"

Thornton smiled. "Yes. I trust that your curiosity will coerce your cooperation."

"Yeah. We'll keep an eye on you, all right. Good-bye, Doc. Good Luck!" He offered his hand.

Thornton accepted it with both hands. "Thank you, and your team, for everything you've done. If it doesn't work out, don't feel bad about it. I've had a good run, and I don't regret anything."

Blake nodded and turned away, unable to say anything further.

8

You still think it's worth it?

Three weeks later, he looked in on his patient. In the darkened room, Thornton was clearly in agony. It took him many minutes to recognize his visitor.

"Thanks for coming, Blake. If I look as bad as I feel, I must look like Hell."

"You do. How bad is it?"

"Hell is a good description. My joints hurt, my muscles hurt, my whole skin is on fire. My teeth have fallen out, what few I had left, and I can't see a damned thing. I can't sleep. I can't rest. I can't get into a position that doesn't hurt, and I can't move without agony. It's Hell, all right."

"Anything I can do for you?"

"The only thing that gives any relief at all, for even an instant, is the cool water I have to drink. It's Hell, but at least I have water."

"You still think it's worth it?"

"I won't know yet, but I'm going to find out. I'll make it to the end, you'll see."

"Good luck, Doc."

"Thanks. You don't have to visit. It doesn't make a difference either way. Come see me at the end."

"I will. You know I will."

Thornton took a sip of water, shaking and trembling as he did.

"Good-bye, Doc."

Thornton said nothing.

9

I'm sleeping in here tonight

"You're doing what?" Ana said into the videophone.

"I'm adopting a son." Alicia repeated.

"Whatever could be the reason?"

"I have some very good reasons. Some day you may learn what they are. Suffice it to say that he needs me, and I like having someone who depends on me."

"Okay. When will I meet him?"

"We'll need a bit more time. The adoption is a bit complicated. I'd guess a couple more months yet. I'll keep you informed. Is Dani still with you?"

"Of course."

"Tell him hi for me. I hope he'll be pleased as well."

"I'm sure he won't be able to contain his joy at becoming a surrogate father."

"That sounds about right. Well, I wanted to let you know, so that you won't be completely surprised when I introduce him."

"In that case, what is the lucky lad's name?"

"We're changing his name to Roni. It's abbreviated in form, like Dani's. He can take credit for that, because we got the idea from him."

"Really? How is that?"

"I'll explain later. I hope to see you soon, and I hope you will be as pleased as I am about this."

"I'll try. Goodbye, sweetheart."

"Goodbye, Love!"

Ana broke the connection. This was so unlike Alicia. Perhaps she was at last becoming more independent. Oh well! A girl has to grow up sometime. Maybe.

She went to find Dani.

* * *

Dani had been invited to come home. He decided to take Ana with him. Perhaps mother would be pleased.

Perhaps father would be pleased!

When they arrived, both he and Ana were the ones who were surprised, for Alicia was already there. She too had a guest. Dani saw a boy about his size, with straight black hair falling in a rather ragged mop. Shy eyes peeked out under his bangs. He smiled.

"Ana, Dani, I'd like to introduce Roni. Roni, this is my niece Ana, and her very good friend Dani."

"I'm very pleased to meet you both." Roni said.

"We changed his name when I adopted him. I liked the way your name was constructed, so I selected this one for the same reason." Alicia said to Dani.

"I'm honored."

"Me too!" Roni said with a grin.

Dani's mother, Rho, approached the group, placing a hand on the head of each young man to ruffle their hair. "I told Roni that you would take him around the neighborhood and give him a chance to stretch his legs. He has definitely been cooped up too long!"

"Sure! We could do that. Would you like to join us, Ana?"

"No way! I'm staying here to find out all your secrets." She smiled.

"Where's Dad?" Dani asked.

"He'll be here later. He said to tell you he wants a report on Roni's baseball skills." Rho answered.

"I'm sure we can do that, if we leave right away."

"You boys go have fun!" Ana kissed Dani. Alicia leaned down and kissed Roni as well.

"Be careful!" Rho called out to them as they departed.

As expected, Dani was able to collect enough players for a game. He and Roni played hard until it was too dark to see. They trudged reluctantly homeward.

"That was fun! It's been a while." Dani said.

"Oh, tell me about it! I got quite a workout."

"That's what I like about it. You have fun, and you build up an appetite. My mom loves to see me eat supper after I've been playing ball."

"That sounds really good!" Roni was grinning hugely through his dirt-stained face.

Dani, of course, didn't get very far before Rho confronted him.

"Hold it, Mister. Off to the bathroom with you. I have a new shampoo for you too."

Alicia glanced over as well. "You too, Roni. Don't stand there dripping dirt all over this nice lady's carpet."

The two ball-players headed for the bathroom.

"Would you mind, Rho? I didn't bring any shampoo with me. Getting used to the shenanigans of a boy is trying."

"It's no problem at all, Alicia. Our bathtub is more than big enough for the two of them. Come along and help, won't you?" At the moment, Rho had not been informed about Roni's special status. To her, this was just another boy like her own.

In truth, she had no doubt about Dani's age. She could compute it easily. But she simply would not accept that he was anything other than what he appeared; a ten-year old boy.

She was not mentally afflicted in any way. It was just more psychologically comfortable for her to treat him that way. Since Dani supported her apparent delusion by acting the role, it was essentially a game they played. Rho was now unaware that others had entered the game.

Dani found the situation a trifle unusual. His mother knew his true age, and Alicia was in on it too. However, his nature was to simply accept a social situation with total equanimity. Roni was a pleasure to be with, and acting like a boy having fun was quite simply a matter of actually doing it.

The two of them relaxed calmly in the tub and allowed the women to see to their cleanliness. It was a common happening for Dani when he visited, and Roni also went along without objection.

Rho and Alicia helped the boys to get dried and to put on short pajamas. Dani's closet offered a sufficiency.

They came to the supper table dressed that way. Dani's father, Blake, was observing them.

"Well boys, who won the game?"

Roni looked up. "We did, I think. Do you remember?" He asked Dani.

"If you mean who had more fun, we definitely did. Roni's a good player, Dad." Dani responded.

"That is just great. I'm pleased that you are enjoying your visit." Turning to Alicia, he asked, "How long will you be able to stay?"

"Now that everyone is here, I'd like to stay for at least a week. Would that be too long?"

"Certainly not! Let's plan on your doing that, then, and if it isn't long enough, we'll extend it later. Okay, boys?"

"Great, dad!" "Thanks, Mister Corrigan!"

Blake smiled.

Ana was observing all this with a controlled curiosity. She knew that machinations were going on, but it wasn't clear at the moment what exactly the plot was. She and her daughter would have a long heart-to-heart soon. In the meantime, she acted the dutiful niece, helping in the kitchen with a smile.

During supper, sleeping arrangements were casually assigned. Ana would sleep in her aunt's designated room, and the boys would bunk together.

In the semi-darkness, the "boys" spoke softly.

"I was surprised to learn that Miss Alicia decided to adopt you. What's your story?" Dani asked rather directly, in the manner of a young boy.

"Well, I'm an orphan. I guess she found out about it and felt sorry for me. When she first came, I was still kinda sick. I hadn't been eating well, and I lost a lot of weight."

"You're pretty lucky. She's a nice lady."

"Yeah. What about you? I notice that Miss Ana gave you a kiss."

"She's sorta my girlfriend. We met at a party. She likes me."

"What do you think we could do tomorrow? I've been cooped up for a long time."

"That's what Mom said. What was wrong with you?"

"It was a degenerative condition. They had to give me a special treatment. It took a long time."

"Oh. How do you feel now?"

"I feel great! I'm ready for anything now."

"Cool. Do you want to go swimming?"

"I sure do!"

"Then that's what we'll do. Tomorrow."

They slept.

In the morning, they were awakened when Ana jumped on the bed. "Hey!" she said.

"Hey, yourself. Good morning." Dani replied.

Ana kissed him.

"Nice." Said Roni.

"I'd like to kiss you too. Do you mind?" Ana asked him.

"No, I don't mind. I'd like that, I think."

Ana kissed him. Then she kissed him again. "Um, I like that too." She said. She pushed his hair back from his eyes and looked at him closely. "You look nice. Very handsome."

"Thank you."

"What are you guys doing today?"

"We talked about swimming." Dani said.

"Good! I'd like to go too."

"Sure. It'll be fun."

"So how long have you been with my Aunt Alicia?" Ana asked Roni.

"Two weeks."

"You should have stopped to visit Dani and me."

Roni eyed the two of them. "Dani stays with you?"

Ana kissed him again. "Yes. I like kissing him."

"I'll bet. I haven't tried it."

Ana looked over at Dani. He shrugged.

"Anyway," Roni said, "I was still recuperating these last two weeks. I didn't feel up to traveling much, and we had to get some stuff for me."

"What kind of stuff?" Ana asked.

"Shoes, clothes, the whole works. I came to her straight out of the hospital, and without anything at all."

"Wow! What did you do, fall out of the orphan truck?" Dani asked.

"Pretty much. I'm doing better now, though."

"Okay, cousin. Let's eat breakfast, and then Dani can take us swimming." She moved over to kiss Dani, and then she left to get out of her nightgown.

"Getting kissed in the morning is nice." Roni said.

"Yep." Dani replied. He got up and got dressed.

The three youngsters placed their clothes in a locker when they got to the indoor pool. After swimming for a while, they took a break on artificial grass under an artificial sun.

Ana sat where she could see the others clearly, and she looked them over carefully.

"You two could be brothers." She said.

"Are you going to start kissing on us again?" Dani asked her.

"Not here. We're not supposed to do that here. It sets a bad example for the children." She answered, "Maybe after we get back home."

That took a few more hours. They returned home with hearty appetites. Ana fixed a plate of salad and fruit.

"Are you having fun?" She asked the boys. They nodded.

"I think I need to wash my hair." She mused.

"We'll help, if you want us to." Dani offered. Roni looked surprised, but nodded in agreement.

"Okay, come on." She led the way into the bathroom. Shortly, after the two boys had done a good job of shampooing her hair, the three of them were involved with lathering and washing and rinsing each other's bodies. It was very merry.

They dried off and went into Dani's bedroom together. Ana sat on the bed. She kissed first one boy and then the other.

"I'm sleeping in here tonight." She said.

"Good!" replied Dani. They looked at Roni.

He shrugged. "I'm okay with it."

"Well, that's not the point," Ana explained. "Dani and I usually sleep together. I'm telling you this not because I don't want you to feel left out, but because I don't want to feel left out."

"I understand. I'll make arrangements to sleep elsewhere."

"No."

"No?"

"No. You'll be here with us, and you won't be just sleeping. You'll be a part of whatever we do."

Dani scratched his head. "Uh … I'm only ten."

Ana kissed him. Then she kissed Roni.

"Now, Roni, you kiss him too."

"What?" the two boys said together.

"Do it." Ana insisted.

Dani looked at Roni and rolled his eyes. Well, he had been a girl for fourteen years. He could reprise the role for a moment. He stood up straight and closed his eyes.

Roni looked at Ana for a moment, and then embraced Dani, planting a kiss squarely on his lips, and lingering over it. Then he stepped back.

"Now kiss me." Ana said.

Roni kissed her in the same manner.

"Which is better?" she asked him.

"Well, you are. No offense, Dani."

Dani shrugged.

"Fine. Now tell me *why?*"

"Well, it may not have looked like it, but you … surrendered … more. It was like you were giving yourself away. Kissing Dani was like kissing … your hand."

"Good. That's a good answer. Now we can proceed with the rest of it. Roni has a secret, Dani."

"No! You can't …" Roni began.

"Yes! You can call it a woman's intuition if you want, but I felt it from the beginning. All the clues were there for me, from Alicia's strange behavior, your interest in this family, and some other subtle things … I know who you are!"

Roni sat down.

Dani was staring from one to the other. Ana looked at him.

"Roni is older than either of us." She said.

"What?!! Really?"

"Yes. You used to know him as … well, you once danced for him."

Dani stared at her, and then looked at Roni, shaking his head. Then he sat down too.

Roni was looking crushed, and shrunken. His slim and youthful body looked puny and shriveled. He sobbed.

Dani looked over at him, and stood before him. He reached out and lifted Roni's face to look at him. Tears had filled the dark-haired boy's eyes.

Dani kissed him again, on his lips and on his eyes, lifting the tears and licking his lips with their taste.

"Welcome home." Dani said. He embraced the shaken boy, and felt thin arms wrap around him in return.

Ana pulled the two of them into an embrace with her as well. The three children stood there for several minutes, just hugging each other and crying.

10

That's a good start

The next morning, the three children behaved as though nothing at all were unusual. They laughed during breakfast, and made plans for the day just as any other youngsters might.

It was a day for sightseeing, and one of the first stops was a cemetery.

"I helped to plot his demise." Roni said.

"I don't think I'd want to kill somebody, even like this." Ana responded.

"I did it once." Dani said cryptically.

They looked at him.

"It was a long time ago. Lori was only five years old. It was one of the earliest times I had been left responsible for her. I had it all under control, and then a burglar broke in."

"Oh, no!" Ana exclaimed.

"Yeah. He was a good-sized fellow too, quite muscular. He probably weighed three times what I did. He may have known somehow that we were there alone. I've heard that sometimes they use computer searches to find their victims. Anyway, he was there to steal from us, but that wasn't all he was there for."

Dani had a distant look on his face, as if he were in a trance. "He seemed especially pleased to be all alone in an apartment with two young girls. Lori was in her bed, not quite realizing what was going on. He ignored her and bound my hands."

Dani looked at his companions. His face seemed a little pale. "He took out a really sharp knife and cut all my clothes off. I got the impression he had done that before. That's when I decided to kill him."

Roni interrupted. "You were naked and bound, in a room with a muscular madman and your five-year old sister, and you decided to kill him? How?"

"Before my parents left me alone with Lori, they made sure I had everything I would need to take care of her. They had purchased a "Nursemaid" robotic arm, and it was installed in the nursery. This was a full-capability unit such as they use in nursing homes to assist with elderly patients, lifting them from the bath and such. It was powerful, but it had been adjusted for dealing with a child's weight."

"Most operators use a console, putting their own arm into a tracking device, and letting the machine interface multiply their strength. Because I had my cybernetic implants, I used that method of controlling it."

"I hadn't used it very often, usually just to carry Lori into the bed if she fell asleep on the floor. But I knew how to use it. I also knew how to reset it to make my own motions more powerful. That's what I did."

"I multiplied its strength up to about twenty times my own, and then I just reached out and grabbed him by the neck and lifted him up. I had to do it quickly before he would hear the arm moving and respond to it. I didn't know how effective my action was going to be until I heard his bones breaking. When I grabbed him, I broke his neck."

Dani turned away from the gravestone. "I used his knife to cut myself free, and then I opened the big round window of the nursery room, which was our bedroom. Using the arm, the "Nursemaid", I simply dragged his body through the window and released it. We were twenty floors up."

"I closed the window and cleaned up the room. I threw away my cut-up clothes and got dressed. Then I made some supper for Lori and myself, and we went to bed."

"You never made a police report?" Ana asked.

"No. I read later that they had found his body, identified him as a

68

known burglar, and concluded that he had fallen before gaining entry to the building. They didn't even notify the residents of the apartment complex, and my parents never knew it happened. This is the first time I ever told anyone."

"You poor kid!" said Roni.

"I was close to thirty. I knew what I was doing. I only looked like a kid. He picked on the wrong kid though, especially when he threatened Lori as well. It didn't even spoil my appetite. Lori doesn't remember anything about it."

"That's a lot more intensive than what I went through. All we had to do was find a physician to write a death certificate."

"When someone who is over a hundred years old drops dead or disappears from sight, people don't ask too many questions."

"So you gave it all up?" Ana said, relieved to be changing the subject.

"A new life." Roni shrugged. "I planned on working back into it gradually, under a new name. Science has always been my love."

"Among other things." Ana added.

"Oh, give it a rest. Haven't I proved myself yet?"

"Not sufficiently, no. I keep seeing you kissing Dani."

"You keep telling me to."

"Are you going to do everything I tell you to do?"

"Pretty much. Yeah."

"Good. That's a good start. Let's go eat something."

"Let's go to Lori's apartment. She should be there, but don't say anything about what I told you. Even now it could probably ruin her sleep."

"Don't worry," Roni said, "that's the kind of story a person should carry to his grave."

They all stopped for a moment, and looked back over their shoulders. Then they laughed.

11

I can't remember me

Lori was at home, and pleased to see them. They introduced her to Roni.

They made themselves comfortable in Lori's tiny apartment. Had they been full-sized, it might have been really cramped.

"I'm glad you came, Dani, and Ana. I have a message for you, from Malcolm."

"A message?"

"He's working out a business deal with several important investors. He needs your go-ahead for the contract."

Dani looked at Ana. She shrugged. Evidently, she was used to such matters.

"I wonder why me?" Dani mused.

"Call up the message, or call up Malcolm, on my computer and ask him. That's all he would tell me."

Dani made the call.

Malcolm responded, looking at the surprisingly young face on the other end of the connection. He blinked. "Dani," he said in almost surprise, "thanks for getting in touch. We're progressing toward our launch date, and we've developed some interesting problems. Would you be interested in being part of the engineering crew?"

It was Dani's turn to be surprised. He had been looking forward to the coming flight, but as guest and spectator. "Of course! But I'm curious. Why me?"

Malcolm brushed his hand through his hair. "It's frustrating! Of the original team, only Wade is available and suitable for space flight. As you know, we lost Professor Thornton, but no one expected him to be able to go with us anyway. I presume you will be able to pass a flight physical?"

"I think so, as long as there's no height requirement." He smiled.

Malcolm answered seriously. "I don't think that's in there. The other requirements are a substantial working knowledge of the engine function and theory, and all aspects of the rocket design. Do you think you could get up to speed on that?"

"I'm sure of it. Let me have a listing of the job requirements, and everything else that you think will help. I'm afraid I haven't quite assembled a résumé yet."

"I'll send it over, along with our submitted literature on the engine design and operation. They seem to think we should have plans and procedures for every possible contingency."

"Ahem. Well, yes, Malcolm. We should." Dani blinked his eyes innocently at him.

At last Malcolm seemed to relax. He smiled. "Thanks Dani. Say hi to your sister for me."

"I'll do that. And I'll give her a kiss, too. 'Bye, Malcolm."

Dani watched as the terminal churned out the documents and files. Then he set them aside. He would access the displays at his own house.

They ate again, and chatted with Lori. She too was looking forward to the space journey, but she had not been offered a position on the crew. For that matter, neither had Ana. But Ana had negotiated her passage as a result of her family investment in the enterprise. Malcolm was not privy to her secret.

* * * * *

Roni was standing in front of the mirror in the early morning light, just staring at his own naked body.

Dani walked up behind him. "What's wrong?"

"I can't remember me." Roni answered. "I know I was this young once, but I can't remember what it was like. It was such a brief period, so long ago."

"Well, you'll have time to explore it this time."

"But I don't know what to do!"

"Do everything! Do anything. Do nothing. What difference does it make?"

"I don't understand."

"Look. I *have* had time to get used to it. A lot of time. Unless you think you picked the wrong age to be, this is perfect for a lot of activities. You're still weak from recuperating, but you're stronger, pound for pound, than many adults. You at least, can lift your own weight. You can climb trees, swing on ropes, ski, hang-glide, go spelunking, diving, anything!"

"I know that. At least I know it intellectually. Somehow, I keep waiting for someone to tell me what to do. I guess that's what I did the first time through, and I must be expecting the same thing now. But now, I don't have a mom and dad to tell me what to do."

Dani grinned. "I'll bet you made your parents very proud." Playfully, he shoved Roni's shoulder. "But you were probably a failure as a ten-year old. You're supposed to explore your limits, break rules, see what you can get away with, and what you'll get punished for."

"Yeah?" Roni responded, "What did you get punished for?"

"I can't remember ever getting punished at all. I got away with murder."

Roni laughed.

Ana walked up behind them and put her arms over their shoulders. She kissed Dani and then kissed Roni. "Why are you two standing here looking so delicious and ignoring me?"

"Roni needs someone to tell him what to do."

"That's easy. You can help me bathe." Ana said. "You both can. Come on! Get busy!"

The bathtub in the Corrigan home was spacious, but this was testing the limits. Alicia looked in on them and shook her head in mock exasperation. Dani and Roni were dutifully shampooing Ana's hair, while she attempted to tickle them with her eyes closed. They dodged her searching hands and giggled delightedly. They were acting more like four-year olds.

Soon enough, the cleanliness of every inch of all their bodies was to Ana's satisfaction, and it came time to exit the tub. They rinsed and dried thoroughly, taking the time to begin planning today's activities.

"Dad has suggested that we go into the main imaging room at Genano Health to display Malcolm's rocket design. That will allow us to see it in a truer scale, so that we might be able to anticipate any service issues." Dani said.

"Despite the memories I have associated with them, I'm looking forward to it." Roni admitted.

"You boys go ahead. I have to coordinate with Alicia about the contracts, and how our businesses will be handled while I'm gallivanting around the Solar System with you two. Plus, I want to design my space suit for the proper feminine appearance."

"Ouch! I just tried to picture Lori in a space suit with the proper feminine appearance, and my libido almost sprang a leak!" Dani said impishly.

Roni laughed, but Ana looked thoughtful.

"You're right. I'll make sure that her space suit design is properly accentuated too."

"You'll be doing the world a favor, Ana. I assume that there will be news coverage of some sort."

"I think Malcolm has consented to robotic cameras aboard. I'll make sure that he remembers to retain editorial control." Giving a quick kiss to each of them, she wrapped a towel around herself and went to get dressed.

Dani and Roni watched her go.

"Why did she wrap up?" Roni asked.

"Feminine allure." Dani responded. Each of the boys shrugged.

12

Thank You Mister Jennison

(Monday, Oct 7, 2142)
Timeline: _____|_____

Rho had a new outfit for Dani to wear to Genano, and one for Roni as well. New athletic shoes, and a pair of running shorts, topped with matching polo shirts in different colors.

Blake looked at the two of them and rolled his eyes. He knew that his wife would never emotionally accept the actual age of their child.

"Ready boys?" He said.

"Yes Sir, Mr. Corrigan!" "Yes, Dad, we're ready."

But their nervousness was obvious in their restless, giggling behavior. Blake sighed.

He signed his troupe in for access to the main viewing chamber, a place designed to make vast amounts of data visible to teams of researchers all at the same time. Normally it was used to display human genomes and for designing the nanobot machines that repaired them.

It occupied almost the entirety of the fourth floor, and they could have gone there rather directly, but Blake wanted to catch up with Rob Jennison before Rob left for a distant conference meeting. He had been told that Rob was in the large central cafeteria.

They walked in to a relatively noisy confusion, as dozens of impromptu meetings and discussions were taking place over coffee and breakfast items.

Blake spotted Rob and began walking over to his table. Halfway there, a surprising silence surrounded them as voices quieted in their wake.

Blake stopped walking and looked back. Everyone was looking at Dani, whom they recognized as his son because Blake was holding his hand. Only at Genano was Dani's story general knowledge, and the middle-aged man who was still a boy was often the subject of speculation.

This was the first time Dani had been presented to them.

Blake looked at his son.

Dani smiled and let go of his hand. He walked over to the nearest table and shook hands with the people there, moving on around the room. The men accepted his handshake, but most of the women embraced him as if he were their own child, smiling at him and kissing him.

Dani thanked them for everything that they had done for him, acknowledging that the miracle that he represented had been wrought by them. He unhurriedly thanked them all, speaking to them as if he had been friends with them for a long time.

At last, Dani returned to Blake and Roni, and they caught up with Rob Jennison. Rob was grinning hugely.

"Dani, you really ought to come around more often! I think you've brightened everyone's day."

"I didn't realize we'd cause such a stir, Rob," Blake said, looking around as the room settled back to its normal hubbub of chatter.

"Well, Dani's one of our major success stories, Blake. At least one that we can acknowledge." He glanced at Roni. "So, you're over here to use the imaging room? I received your files under secure transmission and set them up in there."

"Yes, Dani's working on a rocket project, and we need its display capabilities to work out any snags. But I also wanted to know if you had finished up with the design information for our "Crow" Project."

"Oh, right. Yes. I've gotten that wrapped up for you. The designs are ready for the initial build, prior to testing on tissue samples. I sent you a memo on internal correspondence."

"Great! I hadn't caught up with the memo yet, and I knew you were going to be unavailable for a while. By the way, I'd like you to meet Dani's friend Roni. They're both very avid baseball players."

"Glad to meet you, Roni!" Rob shook hands with the young man, holding his hand for a moment longer while he looked at it carefully. "It looks to me as though you both are getting plenty of exercise and are growing strong and healthy."

"Thank you, Mister Jennison! Thank you very, very much!" Roni responded.

"Well, thanks again, Rob. Have a good trip." Blake hustled the boys away before anything else might get said that would arouse suspicions. The people of Genano were incredibly bright individuals. This was skirting dangerously thin ice.

Genano Health's viewing room was world-famous for its display capacity. Normally used to portray the human genome for study and ostensible repair mechanism development, the image of the rocket ship was relatively trivial to accommodate. They were looking at a full-sized replica made of light, presented to them in a darkened room.

The pads of the feet were nearly a foot high from the floor, and they were ten feet across. Attached to them were the flexible ankle joints which would allow the feet to adjust to variable terrain. Towering above that was a graceful scissor-type arrangement, which would telescope the landing gear out while the rockets were making their final descent thrust. This rocket was meant for landings on other worlds!

Speaking of rockets, the flared bells of the rocket engines were next to see on their sightseeing tour. They too were massive, each more than twenty feet across, arranged in a pattern like the dots on the five side of a die. The center bell was about twenty-five percent larger than the others.

On take-off or landing, these rocket nozzles would be sending out a blistering stream of incandescently hot gases, fresh from heating in the nuclear furnace, and just short of being plasma in their flow patterns.

The thrust power was enormous!

Crew

Captain
Executive Officer
Navigator
Communications
    Anastasia Winthrope
    Lori Corrigan
Engineering
    Malcolm Horowitz
    Wade Finnigan
    Dani Corrigan
    Roni Winthrope

Dani looked around. This was impressive.

He was in the premier display facility in the world, being shown state of the art engineering with X-ray vision.

It was life-size and full-scale. They were rising up through the ship design as if riding a glass elevator up through the physical ship itself. It was growing around them as if they were standing inside a 3-D printing facility as the ship was being sintered together.

This was impressive.

His father and his friend Roni were standing beside him with absolutely awestruck expressions on their faces.

It was almost adequate.

13

DOWNLOAD COMPLETE

As he had done in Professor Thornton's facility buried inside the mountain, Dani let his cybernetic associates help him with the visualization. He tied the visual inputs and his connections to their feed channels into a cohesive imaging structure that rose inside his mind as the display information rolled forward in the facility chamber.

The ship, which was going to be built from these plans, was already taking shape inside his mind, and he was still inside the image of it. Dani had a momentary recursion image of brains inside ships inside brains like a matryoshka set, or Russian nesting dolls. He thought Anastasia might be amused by that image.

Upward they moved, forward in the ship. Storage facilities, maintenance bays, living quarters, ship's stores, the galley and all the intricate plumbing, a chart room designed to be a miniature of this grand imaging facility, and all the structural supports and complex interwoven engineering of the most modern physics and materials science, all kaleidoscoped into a colliding cacophony of shifting rainbows.

They had reached the forward-most part of the ship now, the control cabin or bridge. If the ship were real, when the ship would be made real, the view out the cabin windows would be of blue sky, or dark space.

Dani stood still in silent rapture. Roni stared at him for a moment, comprehending slowly what was happening in Dani's complex brain.

He had seen him work before, and not known then what was going on. Roni had a song snippet that popped into his mind occasionally under circumstances like this; "Ah, but I was so much older then; I'm younger than that now." He didn't know how the rest of the song went, but that part always brought him a smile.

At last Roni understood that Dani had had years and decades to grow confident and familiar with his mind-extending hardware, while on the outside, and to the outside world, he appeared to make no progress or change at all. Roni realized that far from his having a head start and years of research and life-experience in comparison to Dani, it was Dani who had the jump on everyone around him.

Dani looked like a boy, but he was a superman.

Roni smiled. He realized also, that he had made a very wise, a very prescient decision. He stood, perchance, not on the shoulder of a giant, but side-by-side with him.

They began moving down again. Level by level, Dani walked around, as if taking a stroll through the actual ship. He paused at a bulkhead door, staring at it. He looked at the door, and then at the door opening, as if his eyes were micrometers, and he was measuring the fit.

He was measuring the fit.

For thirty years, Dani had been controlling and communicating with his internal devices. They were the ebb and flow of air currents in a familiar house, the sussurance of background noises in a comfortable office. It had always worked exactly the same way, a friendly voice asking questions and offering information.

Until today.

Dani got a message, a text message, written right across his visual field in red letters.

REPORT: DATA INPUT CHANNELS AND DISPLAY PROCEDURES AT MAXIMUM CAPACITY . . . CHOOSE OPTION.

ONE: DEGRADE DISPLAY PARAMETERS
TWO: TERMINATE DISPLAY PROGRAM

THREE: EXPAND CAPABILITY

PLEASE VOCALIZE CHOICE.

Dani stared at the message. In its presence, he felt as though his visual field was narrowing, giving him tunnel vision.

He glanced over at his companions. They were continuing to look around, waiting for him to proceed with his examination of the displayed information.

Dani realized that this choice being offered was a private thing. He would have to choose, but he could also seek advice. The viewing program was not limited by the Genano Health facility; it was being log-jammed inside his own head. Presumably, he had never encountered such a massive download of information before. He frowned.

Terminating the program seemed pointless. At some point he would have to open it up again.

Degrading or downgrading the display parameters also seemed to be unwise. He needed to analyze these plans and verify their accuracy. If what he had noticed a moment ago was any indication, there were errors in the massive file. That door, perhaps because of a change in the hinge specification, would not fit in its doorframe. It wouldn't close properly.

Dani turned to face the outer wall. Softly but clearly he enunciated his choice, just as if he were giving a verbal command to the display room itself.

"Expand capability," Dani said.

INITIATING PROCEDURE
PROTOCOL REQUIRES ADDITIONAL ASSEMBLER FUEL

ACCESSING COMMUNICATIONS

IMPLEMENTED

The displayed information went away. Dani looked around. Nothing much appeared to be happening, but he wasn't sure what was supposed to happen anyway.

He continued moving through the display room, working his way back down through the ship. He was taking his time, and looking at all of the systems as well as he could, trying to get a feel for the scale of the equipment, as well as the manner in which it interacted with the ship's controls and communications. This was a big ship, but the crew size was going to be small.

Dani had a thought; some of the crew were going to be small as well. He smiled.

The door to the display room opened. Light from the corridor spilled inside, washing out the image of the ship, but silhouetting a man in white clothes.

"Doctor Corrigan? Your refreshments are here." He rolled a cart inside and then departed.

Dani and the others made their way back to the entrance. On the cart was a bottle of brandy and three small glasses.

Dani and Roni looked at the beverage, and then looked toward Blake Corrigan.

"What?" Blake said, "I didn't order it."

"Can I have some, Dad? I think I need it." Dani requested.

Corrigan looked at his son. Even in the strange lighting of the display room, he looked slightly pale.

"Well, why not? We're celebrating something anyway." Corrigan opened the bottle and filled three glasses.

"To space flight!" Blake raised his glass.

"And youth!" Roni added, lifting his glass also.

"And us!" said Dani, "God bless us, every one!"

"Hear, hear!" Blake responded. They clicked glasses and drank.

"Ah, that does taste ... wonderful!" Roni said, sipping cautiously.

Dani emptied his glass, and reached to fill it again.

"Dani, I don't believe I've ever seen you touch alcohol before," his father said mildly.

"This, sir, is processing fuel." Dani looked up with a smile. "I am doing an inordinate number of intensive calculations." He poured a second generous helping.

"Well, hmm," Blake said, "this could be interesting." He looked at Roni, who shrugged, and sipped again.

Dani strolled back into the midst of the display, sipping on his portion more sedately.

Ten minutes later, Dani got a second display message.

SECONDARY PROTOCOL INITIATED
ACCESSING EXPANSION PROCEDURE
DOWNLOADING

Dani felt as if his head had become a communications hub. He could almost hear the data traffic colliding and coursing through his inputs. Was the imaging information from Malcolm being recorded inside his own brain? Momentarily, he felt a little flushed. He continued to wander, and to sip.

After perhaps another half-hour, Dani got a final message:
DOWNLOAD COMPLETE

He turned to his father once more. "I think I've seen enough for now, Dad. Should we go now?"

"Are you ready, Roni?" Corrigan asked the other boy.

Roni nodded, with a smile. This was exciting, but he had had enough of it for now, and did not want to fall asleep in the middle of so much excitement.

Blake compressed and extracted the information again, and collected the storage medium once more. It was, after all, proprietary.

He also picked up the bottle with the remaining brandy. "I have a feeling that I paid for this, so I might as well take it with me."

Dani looked at him.

"Okay, with us," he said, "you can have more if you want it."

Dani smiled. Taking Roni's hand, he led them out into the bright light of the corridor again.

Making their way out of the building once more proved easier than going in had been. They saw very few people.

14

At least it's good brandy

Back at home, Blake studied his son, "Dani, stand still and close your eyes."

Dani stood up straight and closed his eyes.

"Now touch your nose with your right index finger."

Dani touched his nose.

"And now your left index finger," his father instructed.

Dani did as he was told.

"Now turn," Blake commanded him.

Dani realized that his father was testing his sobriety. He suppressed laughing outright, and executed a graceful ballet spin, stopping after a full revolution exactly where he was at its beginning.

Blake blinked. "Well, I guess everything's okay, then. You can open your eyes."

Dani opened his eyes and smiled.

Blake shook his head in puzzlement.

Dani reached for the bottle of brandy, more than half-empty already, which Blake had placed on a small table. "May I?" Dani inquired, raising his eyebrows, "I'm still manipulating those images."

Blake looked up toward the ceiling. "Well, all right, but don't make yourself sick."

Dani smiled, and took off for his room. "Come on, Roni. I want to talk about the rocket!"

"I'll keep an eye on him, Mister Corrigan." Roni said.

"Thanks, Roni. I wish I knew what was going on."

Dani was standing at the window, looking out over the starkly utilitarian cityscape. The brandy bottle was in his hand, but he had not opened it.

"You're scaring your father, you know," Roni said.

Dani looked around. "It's so much to take in."

"What do you mean? You don't have to build it."

"I feel like I do," Dani replied, "have to build it, that is."

"What?"

"It's incomplete," he looked at Roni. "Malcolm may have paid for it, but he might have had the wrong people doing it."

"I think I'm more of an engineer than you are," Roni said slowly. "I didn't see anything wrong."

Dani watched him for a moment. "Oh, yeah. I forgot. You worked with Malcolm for a long time. Were you part of the rocket design team too?"

Roni glanced aside. "No, to be honest. I was only involved with the power production. The rest of it seems challenging, but it's a rather simple design, actually. The fusion generators produce heat and electrical energy, which converts the reaction mass to a working rocket exhaust."

Dani nodded. "I think they must have organized into working groups, committees and such. It's too much for one person to grasp all at once." He looked out the window again.

Roni waited. "Is that what you're trying to do? To be that one person?"

Dani looked at him, and smiled.

Roni came over and gently took the bottle from him. To Dani's amusement, he drank a sip directly.

"That won't help, you know," Dani said.

"Worth a try." Roni replied. "At least it's good brandy."

"It's a little strong for me," Dani answered.

"Then why are you drinking it?"

Dani looked at him. "It's what I told Dad. Assembler fuel."

"What are you assembling?"

"More capability?"

"You don't know?" Roni asked.

"I don't know what the end result will be. I don't expect to be smarter. I'm hoping I'll be able to visualize the whole thing better. That's what I need."

Roni passed the bottle back. Dani drank.

"I think I'll study the engineering drawings and procedures for a while. Maybe that will help." Dani said.

"I'll go get some sandwiches."

"You don't have to stick around," Dani said, "This could be a little boring."

"I wouldn't miss it for the world." Roni answered, "I have the feeling you're going to do something amazing," he smiled, "*again!*"

Dani grinned. "Sandwiches sound like a good idea." He climbed onto the bed and spread out his study documents.

Hours later, the sunlight was fading. Roni looked over from the computer game he was playing, and saw that Dani had fallen asleep.

Roni cleared away the papers and stacked them in an orderly fashion. Then he lay down beside Dani and relaxed with him. The bottle, needless to say, was now empty.

15

Don't get your hopes up

(Tuesday, Oct 8, 2142)
Timeline: _____|_____

D ani was on the verge of waking up when he got a message from an entirely new entity. It came in as voice, but seemed to flow in an extremely condensed and rapid-fire manner.

"Dani, this is White Fang. I have some information to report."

"Go ahead."

"Good Morning. I am the voice of your new enhanced capability. The download you received yesterday has been implemented in its initial stages, and my presence is the result."

"Initial stages?" Dani queried.

"Yes. MIL-SPEC-AP is a specialty program, developed by Genano Health in concert with Military Programs and needs. It was designed to augment the abilities of operatives working with government special agencies and security forces."

"Wait, how did I get it?"

"You asked for it."

"When did I ask for a military special program?" Dani asked.

"Yesterday. You were utilizing a graphic display procedure, and your cybernet determined that it was not up to the task. Accordingly, your machine-level request resulted in accessing the only program upgrade with the enhanced capability to meet the specified parameters."

"Is this something my father was working on?"

"No. Your father does not have the required security clearance to be a part of the MIL-SPEC-AP program."

"And I do?" Dani expostulated.

"No. You are not authorized to work on the program either. Both of you have already been colonized by nano-assemblers. You are prevented from being in the development path for classified programs."

"Then why am I a part of it?"

"You are not involved as a developer. You are involved as an agent."

"Oh." Dani said, "Anything else?"

"That completes my report for now. It is time for you to wake up. You have just been kissed."

Dani opened his eyes. Roni's face was about three inches above his own.

"Hi." Dani said, "Did you just kiss me?"

"Uh-huh." Roni replied, "You were sleeping pretty good. I tried talking to you, and then I shook your shoulder, but you kept sleeping." Roni smiled.

"You have a very lovely innocence in your facial expression when you're sleeping, so I figured, *Sleeping Beauty*, and I gave you a kiss. I guess it worked."

Dani reached up and held Roni's face in his hands. Then he kissed Roni.

"Hmm," said Dani, "just checking to see what it felt like; not very impressive. Kissing you is like kissing my sister." He rolled over and sat up.

"Oh," said Roni, then he looked up, "Oh?"

Dani grinned. "Don't get your hopes up. I like you, but kissing girls is much better."

"I think so too, but you were closer."

"You're a dirty old man. Let's get a bath, and eat something. I'm hungry!"

They were sitting in the breakfast nook, eating cereal, and dressed only in their underwear, when Ana joined them.

"You are both looking very suspiciously innocent," she said. "Why do I have the feeling that you are plotting some mischief?"

"Because you know us?" Roni answered.

Dani grinned.

Ana kissed each of the boys, and prepared cereal for herself as well.

"Did you finish your space suit design?" Roni asked.

"I have a concept." Ana responded, "We'll have separate suits for being in the ship, which will keep us comfortable. They're form fitting and have heating and cooling features, plus a slick surface to repel dirt or spilled substances. That will also let us shimmy into our exterior suits quickly if we need to."

"And," Dani said, "they will make you look good on camera, being form-fitting. I'll bet they don't even have pockets."

Ana looked at him archly. "Of *course* they won't have pockets. How can you reach inside your pocket when you put your outside suit on? These are more like long-johns or pajamas."

"Made to accentuate your appearance too, I suppose?" Dani smiled.

"Yours too, lover!" She gave him a kiss.

Dani smacked his lips. "Yep, definitely sweeter." He looked at Roni.

"That's the cereal you're tasting," Roni pointed out.

Ana looked from one face to the other, "What?"

"Roni woke up his Sleeping Beauty partner with a kiss this morning."

"I'd guess you both were sleeping beauties. *I* should have been kissing you."

"Kissing *us?*" asked Dani.

"Yes, of course, both of you. And tickling you as well." Ana replied, "What good is it to wake someone up if you can't make them giggle?"

"Good." Dani said, "I want us to be comfortable together. Not jealous or anything."

"Why?" Ana asked.

"Because we're going to be on a ship together. We'll *have* to get along."

"Oh, yes. How did the ship look? The images, I mean."

Dani looked to the side. "I'm not finished yet."

"Of course," said Ana, "I'm not finished with my work either."

"Put extra heaters in the suit, and make the slick surface something like Teflon, so it will be acid resistant."

"Okay, why?" said Ana.

"We have to think about potential destinations. We'll be in space, but we might actually end up – somewhere." Dani was looking thoughtful.

"Noted," Ana replied. "We should be getting together with Malcolm at his place in about ten days. Do you think you'll have some information about the ship by then?"

"I think so," Dani said softly. "It's hard to be precise, because I'm still putting things together, but that should work."

"I'm going to recommend to Alicia that she let Roni stick with you for awhile. Maybe he can help you stay focused on the ship design. Malcolm seems to have a lot of confidence in your judgment for some reason. He never even mentions your apparent age."

Roni looked thoughtful. "Malcolm is young himself. I don't think he worries about it. With him, results count, and Dani impressed him. He impressed all of us."

"No kissing him at the breakfast table, Roni. I'm eating," Ana said.

Roni blushed.

16

Ten seconds? It seemed longer

(Wednesday, Oct 9, 2142)
Timeline: _____|_____

"Up and at 'em, soldier. This is White Fang. It's 0600. Time to start your military morning."

Dani did not move. "What in the *hell* are you talking about? You'd better behave while you're inside my head or I'll start beating you with a wooden spoon."

"You'll just get a headache. Don't you want to start getting stronger and preparing for your mission?"

"No, and what mission?" Dani would have blinked, but his eyes weren't open.

"You've been upgraded with a MIL-SPEC-AP. You're in a program to be either a super-soldier or a special agent."

"I think you've slipped a cog. Have you taken a look at your raw material recently?"

"Yes," White Fang admitted, "and I wanted to talk to you about that. You don't fit the program parameters very well. I don't mean to make you feel bad, but you're not exactly soldier material."

"That much I knew already. Why did you think I was supposed to be a soldier?"

"MIL-SPEC-AP. They don't give it to just anybody."

"Well, they gave it to me!"

"All right. The other alternative is to prepare you as a special agent. Perhaps that is the reason that a person with the appearance of a ten-year-old has a MIL-SPEC-AP download."

"You seem rather single-minded about this."

"At the moment, yes. Unless you want to count your mind and my mind as two minds."

"You don't have a mind," Dani said, "You're a program."

"Okay, it's just your mind then. So if anyone is single-minded, it is you."

"What kind of nonsense is that?"

"Tactics. I run through various choices within my program parameters to select the best fit."

"Well, one thing I don't fit is being a soldier." Dani said.

"Okay, special agent it is. That's actually a good choice, considering how puny you are."

Dani took a deep breath. "Puny?"

"You heard me, maggot. You still have training to do, and you've wasted ten seconds already."

"Ten seconds?" Dani said. "It seems longer."

"Ah. This form of communication is faster than normal. I'm already in your head."

"Oh." Dani reflected. "What does a special agent have to do?"

"My guess is you'll be a spy. You'll find ways to get into places other investigating agents won't have access to."

"Yeah, that's a good plan. I can see where a kid would never attract attention in all those secret government institutions. Totally invisible."

"I can't do that yet. I'll do what I can with the limited material I have." White Fang said.

"I like that you have a sense of humor. This could be entertaining."

"Okay, let's go through our list then. I'll increase your strength without changing your basic body form, since you're not following the soldier's path."

"You'd better not change my form! It has taken me years to develop it."

"All right. Next, your imaging capability will be enhanced, of course, that's the whole reason for the download. That will require the development of a quad-core metabionic tanglenet system inside you."

"Of course," Dani said. "Go on."

"Your visual spectrum will be expanded, mainly on the infra-red and higher radio frequencies. You might not be able to hear the broadcasts, but you should be able to see the glow of the transmission."

"Cool! You may continue."

"All right. Vision and memory will be linked to your new visualization capability. In a darkened room, sequential photons will build an image, like a military starlight scope. Infra-red will tie into that, too."

"You'll have a photographic memory, of course," White Fang continued. "Your hearing will be ampanded."

"Wait, what's that?"

"Amplification and expansion. It's the way some microphones work. In your ears, the rush of blood noise will be silenced, and distant sounds amplified. This only helps in relative silence, of course. You could tune in on a specific frequency if you needed to."

"Okay."

"Your olfactory receptors will be tunable, allowing you to focus on a scent like a well-trained dog."

"How flattering."

"How useful! It would let you trail someone in the dark."

"Oh. Yeah, that would be cool."

"Taste we don't tamper with, but touch; well, that depends on skin, and your skin will have to be modified."

"Wait, now. Modified how?"

"We'll make it more damage resistant and less sensitive to heat and cold. We'll put tough fibers under your skin to act as a woven net to prevent penetrations and lacerations. This will tie into your synthetic muscles to allow for better impact absorption, and improved kinetic packaging."

"Whatever that is. I guess I'll find out." Dani said. "Synthetic muscles?"

"Plastic, essentially. We'll grow them alongside your existing muscles, and below them as well. They're more compact than biological tissue, and work faster too. They run on electricity, which we'll set you up to manufacture by absorbing motion energy. That's tied to the modifications to your bones and joints, of course. No sense having strong muscles and weak bones."

"It sounds like I'm going to become a robot!"

"A cyborg, actually; Cybernetic Organism. You're already part-way there, with your implants and device mechanisms. This just allows you to control more powerful machines inside your body, the way you've occasionally done it with external devices."

"Are you sure this isn't the soldier's path?"

"You'll know when you see a soldier. They'd make about five of you."

"Oh." Dani said. "I guess I was getting carried away with these new capabilities."

"Well, console yourself with the fact that soldiers don't normally get the full gamut of enhancements like this. It would complicate their mission to have too many input variables. Espionage agents, on the other hand, need all the input variables they can acquire."

"That seems to make sense." Dani mused.

"It's going to take a few days to get it set up. You may notice a little strangeness in your appetite. I'll need the energy and the raw materials."

"What will I need to do?"

"Just go on with your normal activities. In fact, you'll need to learn to mask these abilities, so that no one knows you have them. The most important part of espionage is maintaining your cover and being able to blend into the background."

"Well, that should certainly be no problem. I'll simply give a quick smile and wave just before I blast off into space."

"Space?"

"Yeah, you know, rocket ship? The reason I needed the upgrade in the first place?"

"Oh." White Fang paused. "It occurs to me that this combination of circumstances was not properly planned."

"Ya think?" Dani exclaimed. "I don't remember planning any of this!"

"Okay. I seem to have my directions and procedures squared away. I'll report back when I have new information."

"All right," Dani said. "What time is it?"

"Just a few seconds before six oh one. Are you getting up?"

"All that in one minute?" Dani said. "I'm going back to sleep!"

"Aye, Captain."

"I like it better when you're saluting than when you're ordering me around."

"Don't worry. I'll put you through your paces soon enough, maggot. And the pace will be breathtaking. But I've got work to do right now. I'll see you later."

"Thanks, White Fang." Dani said sleepily.

17

I call it the Cottage Garden

(Tuesday, Oct 15, 2142)
Timeline: _____|_____

Dani and Roni stepped out of the travel car at their destination, only to discover that it wasn't their planned destination at all.

Instead of the public platform near Malcolm's mountain retreat, this appeared to be a sunny tropical park.

They were standing on a flat section of rock that constituted a natural patio surface. Behind them, a moss and ivy-covered rock face obscured the opening where they had exited. There was no indication of a seam in the rock.

Dani looked up. What he had taken for an open sky proved to be an arch of supporting latticework, with bright lights making it difficult to see the structure. This was an artificial space, and it could have been anywhere.

Dani looked over at his companion. Roni clearly did not know where he was either.

Scanning over the scene once more, Dani began working his way down toward the lower level, where water could be heard gurgling softly.

Roni followed him. It didn't seem likely that they would become separated even in this cavernous volume, but an unspoken apprehension grew around them.

They walked through an airy, garden-like space, with fruit trees, grape vines and berry bushes lining the path. It was quiet and warm.

A picturesque arched wooden bridge led them over a tumbling brook, which emptied into a placid pond. On the side of the pond, a crude diving board was secured in heavy boulders.

At length they came to a tiny cottage, surrounded by a low picket fence with an opening, but no gate. At a shaded table in the yard, a girl was reading a book, and sipping tea.

They stopped at the entrance. She looked up at them, and gestured them inside with a smile.

She appeared to be between sixteen and seventeen, relatively dark of complexion, with a pixie-style haircut of extraordinarily black hair. She had startlingly piercing eyes. Though smiling, she looked at them as if she were seeing right through them.

She wore an embroidered, peasant-style blouse over a dark sleeveless pullover, and knit shorts. Her feet were bare.

"Hi!" She smiled, and put down her book; "Backyard Vegetable Gardening".

"Hello. I'm Dani. This is my friend, Roni."

"I'm Selena," she said, "Would you like some tea?"

"Yes, Please!"

"Have a seat." She got up and went into the cottage.

In a moment, she returned with a small tray.

The boys busied themselves with preparing their cups, while Selena freshened her own drink. She made a curious gesture with her hand, as if using it to wave away the rising steam from her tea. Then she looked at her empty hand and smiled.

Dani took a sip. "That's very good! Thank you!"

She nodded.

"Selena," Dani looked around. "You live here?"

She followed his glance. "I like it here. It's usually very quiet."

"You're alone here?" Dani asked mildly.

"Not any more!" She smiled brightly, as if having made a clever observation.

"You aren't afraid?" asked Roni.

She looked him over. "Not to injure your male ego, but as petite as I am, I still make two of you." She smiled again, to soften the words. "No, I'm not afraid."

"Where is this?" Dani asked.

"I call it the Cottage Garden," Selena answered.

"That's a good name. Where is it?" Dani persisted.

She shrugged.

"You don't know? How did you get here?"

"How did *you* get here?" she returned.

"We weren't coming here. We were going somewhere else, and then, we were here." Dani finished with a lame shrug.

"That's how it was for me too." Selena said.

"How long have you been here?" Roni asked.

"It's been a long time; A few years … I was twelve when I started. I kinda grew up here."

"Oh, wow!" Roni exclaimed.

Dani looked at him. Then he looked at Selena. "So it's like a prison, then?"

"I guess it's like a prison, but it's not like punishment." She looked at him with a dauntingly direct stare. "What are you in for?"

Wanting to squirm under the power of her gaze, Dani smiled instead, and shrugged. "I don't know."

She raised her hands. "See how it is?"

"Maybe we should look around."

"You should look around." Selena said, "When you come back, if I'm inside, come on in."

"Thanks!" said Roni.

Casually, the boys made their exit, looking around as if interested in everything about the cottage.

Out the gate, they turned toward the direction they had not come from, and began walking.

There wasn't a road, so much as a path, meandering through the park-like surroundings. They observed that in back of the cottage was a substantial garden, well tended and apparently productive.

They continued along the path, coming into what appeared to be a casual orchard. Apple and pear trees gave way to a citrus grove, where oranges decorated the small trees like Christmas decorations.

Berry bushes snaked their way along sinuous paths, seemingly designed to encourage nibbling as one walked. The whole valley was truly a garden.

"What do you think we've gotten into?" Roni asked after a bit, sorting through a handful of berries.

"It seems pretty obvious that we've been kidnapped."

"Kidnapped?" Roni looked startled. "What makes you say that?"

"Someone went to a lot of trouble to redirect the public transit system to a hidden location, and we're locked in here as effectively as at any secure facility. Do you know the way out?"

Roni looked back the way they had come.

"No, that wouldn't work, or we could have left again as soon as we arrived. That was a one-way door, or at least one we can't open from this side."

"I didn't think about that."

"Think about this," Dani continued, "only the government has the connections to pull off something like this. I think we're here to be interrogated."

"Interrogated?" Roni twisted his face into bafflement. "What have we done to get in trouble with the government, or a government?"

"I can't be sure, but I think it has to do with that drunken bender we went on the other day."

"Drunken bender? We can't get drunk, and you hogged all the brandy anyway."

"True," Dani replied, "but why was I drinking?"

"You said it was assembler fuel." Roni looked closely at him. "What aren't you telling me?"

"I got an upgrade." Dani said slowly. "I think it was almost accidental. Maybe I wasn't supposed to receive it, and the government is now trying to figure out either how they can take it back or maybe draft me into service somehow."

"Draft you into service? What could they use you for?"

"What would you use me for, if you had the control?" Dani looked his friend in the eye.

Roni's eyes widened.

"Yeah, see? It doesn't take a lot of imagination to get creepy in a hurry, does it?" Dani said gravely. "They set me up to be a secret agent."

"You're a spy?" Roni looked puzzled, "for whom"

"That's the mystery, isn't it?" Dani grinned. "They equipped me to be a spy, but they didn't put me into any organization. My problem is, I can't figure out how they could use a boy to be a spy anyway. They're probably looking at it the same way."

He stopped to gather a few berries himself.

Roni was working his way through the implications. "So this place, they're going to hold you here, hold us here I guess, until they figure out what to do with you."

Dani nodded.

"And I'm just collateral damage?"

Dani smiled. "That's up to you. How would you like to join my army?"

"Your army? What army?"

"You and me; a secret agent team, working together. We'd be more effective as a team, and that way you wouldn't be considered a threat to security with no additional value to them. It's a way to *avoid* your being just collateral damage."

"But how could you "equip" me to be a spy too?"

"I still have the download information. All it does is provide an upgrade to your existing genomic nanobot programming. That's what it did to me. I've been remade into a secret agent with special abilities. You could have them too."

"Do you think it would work?"

"I don't see how it would fail to work." Dani looked at him, "You've already had much more extensive changes imposed on you. Do you notice anything different about me since my upgrade?"

"Not really, no. Are you saying that it's painless?"

"It's not without side-effects, that's true. I don't even know if there is pain involved. I haven't felt any. I think one of the changes is pain management. That would probably be one of the first things modified."

"I went through," Roni closed his eyes and drew a few calming breaths, "… a lot of pain with my last transformation." He opened his eyes. "I hope you're right that it won't hurt again."

"Hang on a minute," Dani said, as he found a place to sit down. "I need to consult with my program." He closed his eyes.

Roni watched him for a moment, then walked around gathering more food. Remembering the brandy incident, he assumed that he would need some processor fuel himself. Besides, the berries were quite tasty.

18

Another puny little superman

"White Fang, I may have a mission for you."

"You idiot! Don't you know anything about Operational Security?"

"No, actually, but I'd like an honest evaluation of my current situation and your advice on how I should proceed. Take your time and tell me what I should do."

"Yeah, I can see how it might look to you. You think you're maneuvering to take control of your only assets in an unfamiliar and threatening environment. But I find it hard to accept that the first thing you do is blow your cover. Roni didn't have to be dragged into this too, and now you've put him in the same situation you're in."

"That's the point. He's already in a compromised position. And I'm going to need all the help I can get. Besides, at least I can trust him."

"What makes you think you can trust him?"

"He's my friend."

"That kind of evaluation is not in my programming."

"Trust me."

"Yeah sure. That makes sense. I told you that kind of evaluation is not in my programming."

"You'll do. What do I need to do to bring Roni into MIL-SPEC-AP?"

"I'm not authorized to do that."

"Yes, you are. I'm authorizing you. We're on a field mission, deep in unknown territory, and I need to augment my resources. I'm ordering you to upgrade Roni with the MIL-SPEC-AP program the same way it works for me."

"All right. I'll need to gain access to his genome pattern and his current nanobot population. Then I'll need to modify his nanobots to work like yours but with his form as their base. After that, we'll build a separate quad-core metabionic tanglenet system inside him that can communicate with you, and then we'll download the program. In a few days, he'll be another puny little superman just like you."

"Okay, that sounds like a good plan. How do we gain access to his genome pattern and nanobot population?"

"Easy enough. Why don't the two of you just swap spit for a few minutes? You do know how to French kiss, don't you?"

"That comes from your programming?"

"I've been influenced by my environment. Is there a problem?"

"I can work with it. Do me a favor though. Don't call him maggot. You can call him rookie. Remember that he's my friend."

"Friend and lover, from my point of view."

"White Fang, one day you're going to teach me how to kill people, aren't you?"

"You can do that now. One day I'll teach you how to do it with finesse."

"Yeah. Looking forward to that. All right, let's get started then. Prepare for MIL-SPEC-AP, Roni version."

Dani opened his eyes, and shuddered slightly.

o-o-o

"So, Roni, I think we have a plan."

Roni looked around, his hand full of berries. "That was quick. I thought you'd be out of it for a while."

"No, internal communication is pretty fast. My program and I have worked out a procedure. We're going to download the Application into you, and give you the same upgrades that I got. You'll be as capable a secret agent as I am in a few days. Then we'll make a great team."

Roni stared out through the garden space. "Are you sure this is the only way?"

"Truthfully no. I'm not sure about anything. Maybe I'm just being paranoid. All I can think is that we're in a place we're not supposed to be, and I don't know what can be done about it."

"This could be a drastic step." Roni looked at him. "You're possibly in trouble because you've accessed information and capacities you're not authorized to have, and now you're considering compounding the error by expanding the list of people who aren't authorized to have it."

"Doubling it, actually." Dani replied. He shrugged. "I don't know if the two of us together would be more of a capability or more of an annoyance factor. At the moment, though, it's the only thing I can think to do that might actually give us more control. Presumably we can do more together than we can separately."

Roni stared, thinking. "This would link us together even more strongly, wouldn't it?"

Dani nodded. "Much more strongly." He said softly.

"Inseparable?"

Dani shrugged. "Buddies, maybe. My application agent said he considered you my friend and lover. Not that I agreed with him about that."

"Friends at least then. As to the other, you seem flexible but not necessarily *that* flexible."

Dani chuckled. "The bonding process requires us to do some kissing."

Roni watched him. "And?"

Dani shrugged. "I'm flexible, I guess."

Roni grinned. "I'll try to be gentle."

Dani laughed. "Just kissing for now, remember?"

"For now. Okay. Ana is going to be disappointed."

"No she's not. We're doing this so we can get back with her."

"Let's hope it works." Roni sighed. "The things I go through for your fantasies."

Dani faced him. "We might as well start. The first step is to analyze your current nanobot genetic sequence in order to redesign your pattern and the devices that control it. Mine got modified by a download, but yours will have to be modified by my version."

"You're going to make me pregnant, I just know it," Roni complained.

"Shut up and kiss me, before I chicken out."

Then they kissed; a long, slow, lingering kiss. Dani tried to concentrate on how it had been to kiss Ana this way.

"That's sufficient," White Fang said inside Dani's head, "unless you perverts want to get even more disgusting."

"I may need to reprogram your attitudes too, White Fang. Just remember this is a military operation and soldier on." Dani responded to the voice inside his head.

They broke off. Roni continued standing still with his eyes closed.

"All right, old man; back to business. Lacking a source of alcohol, we'll have to make do with fruit sugar. Let's start packing on the calories."

Roni looked down. He still had a handful of berries. He began eating them as they turned to proceed further into the chaotic order of their paradise.

Hours later, Dani realized that despite the observably small size of their prison, it was still possible to wander around it finding new and unfamiliar locations.

And it was growing dark.

They decided to camp out for the night. With all the easily available eats, they wouldn't need to cook anything, so they had no need for a campfire.

Dani found a small hollow space and gathered some dry leaves for them to nest in. They settled down and cuddled together.

In the darkness, Dani was awakened by a voice inside his head. "White Fang reporting. The initial build for the Roni project is ready."

Dani rolled slightly onto his back He brushed some leaves out of his face and took a deep breath.

"Can't you wait until morning?" He said silently.

"It is morning. It's 2:30 in the morning. You've been sleeping for nearly four hours."

"Can't it wait until daylight anyway? Such daylight as we may get anyway."

"It's best if we start as soon as possible. However, I had a question or two. Among the many genome patterns available I found a confusion of what I assume to be plant materials as well as human. Did you want the Roni Project to include fruit flavors and sugars?"

"Now I know this is just a nightmare. Why in hell would I want Roni to have plant materials in his genome?"

"In the sample genetic information from your shared saliva, I found several varieties of plant sugars. I was asking if you wanted to incorporate any plant capabilities into the genomic patterns we will be using in the Roni program the way bird DNA was used for Selena."

"Look, we were eating berries when you had us start kissing. That's where the plant material came from." Dani blinked mentally. "Wait a minute. What bird DNA are you talking about?"

"I found a few cells in your saliva that didn't match either you or Roni, or even the food you had eaten. I'm assuming it came from Selena. You were using her dishes after all, and talking with her."

"Yeah but she's not a bird."

"She's certainly not a chicken. I've seen that in your diet recently, from eggs and fried chicken you've eaten. But I recognized the DNA in her cells as being avian. It's not a lot, but she definitely has some of it in her cells."

"Huh. I have no idea what any of that means. What about the plant cells, the berry flavors?"

"It was in your saliva. I was just asking if you wanted to utilize it in the Roni genome build."

"Utilize it how? You want him to grow leaves or something?"

"No, you don't need photosynthesis for collecting energy. I have other means for that. I was just asking if you wanted the Roni project to have a particular aroma, or to generate varieties of flavor in the various exudates."

Dani had a horrific vision for a moment; of Roni oozing some syrupy sweetness and wanting to be licked clean of it. He shuddered at the thought, although it occurred to him that Ana might not entirely share his misgivings about it.

"Look," Dani said mentally, "don't change his genome from what it is any more than you need to for the MIL-SPEC program. If you want to store the data, go ahead and do that, and maybe we can come back to ways to use the information somehow."

"Ah, a reference database. I could support it as an addendum to the quad-core metabionic tanglenet system, and add to the database as we come across more examples of chimeric applications."

"Okay, fine, do that. I thought you said you were ready to download the changes to Roni."

"Storage is easy. Integrating into a genome is more difficult. Luckily you and Roni have matching genomes for the most part. It's almost as if he were patterned after you. The download is ready, and all the information needing to be stored has been packaged."

"All right. How do we deliver the package?"

"A variety of options are available, but for now the package has been prepared as a bit of phlegm in your saliva. All you have to do is place it in his mouth."

"You really are a sick military bastard, White Fang. Do you know that?"

"I suppose I should take pride in my training, but it's actually only programming. Are you ready?"

"All right. Now what?"

"Just clear your throat and place it on your finger, then put it into Roni's mouth. Against the cheek will do. If you cause him to choke he might wake up."

"You are so nasty. All right, let's do it." Dani shifted around, preparing Roni, who was still asleep. He cleared his throat and produced something he could spit out onto his finger. Carefully he separated Roni's lips and slipped the unpleasant "package" inside Roni's mouth.

Roni shifted uneasily, but settled down again and remained asleep.

Relaxing, Dani looked up into the darkened sky, where "stars" shifted slightly under the influence of air currents. For a moment he thought he saw a shadow of something, but it could have been his imagination. Dani rolled over and wrapped himself around Roni once more.

In minutes, he was asleep again.

19

I didn't get much company

(Wednesday, Oct 16, 2142)
Timeline: _____|_____

All too soon, Dani was rudely awakened again. It had started to rain. Dani sat up. Beside him, Roni stirred as well.

"It's raining." Roni observed. He blinked. "The rain is cold."

Dani sighed. "Come on, let's get back to Selena's house. It can't be too far."

"But it's pitch black out. I can't see a thing!"

"Take my hand. I'll guide us." Dani pulled his companion to his feet and they set off through the forest.

Ten minutes later, they were trudging through Selena's gate and taking shelter on her small porch.

Selena opened the door. Staring at the two of them with some bemusement, she ushered them inside.

"It was raining," Dani said a little lamely as he stood dripping on the floor.

"It always rains at four in the morning."

"Oh. I didn't know that." Dani responded softly.

"Come on. Get a quick shower and give me your clothes to wash. Then you can sleep here on the couch. I'll set out a quilt for you."

The boys went into the bathroom together and followed her instructions. Dani handed her all of their clothes. Smiling softly, Selena accepted them from him.

They showered quickly and dried off, each wrapping his towel around himself afterwards.

Dani led them back into the main room, where a quilt had been draped over the couch. Dani put his towel over the back of a kitchen chair and got in position on one end of the couch, wrapping the quilt around himself. Roni repeated his actions and settled in on the other end.

Dani could hear a washing machine running in the distance, but he was asleep before he saw Selena again.

0-0-0

Dani opened his eyes. Selena was sitting at the table, sipping a cup of tea and watching him. The towels were gone and the room was neat and tidy again.

Dani sat up and stretched his arms, and looked around. Selena watched him with her intensely piercing gaze while he did so.

"You still have tea?" Dani said softly.

Selena nodded and rose to get him a cup.

Returning to the table, Selena said casually, "Your shoes are out on the porch rail, where the sun can shine on them. I washed all of your clothes and they are hanging out on the line to dry."

"Thank you. You have been very hospitable."

Selena pushed the cup closer to his side of the table, smiling softly in invitation.

It was a dare and a challenge. Dani moved the quilt aside and stood up. Unhurriedly, he walked to the table.

She watched him very closely as he moved. "I don't get much company."

Sitting down, Dani picked up his cup and cautiously sipped it. "It's still good tea."

"I'll fix you some breakfast when your friend wakes up."

"You're very kind."

"I was thinking about making you work it off." Selena said rather softly.

"What did you have in mind?" Dani sipped his tea.

As if making up her mind, Selena looked him in the eye. "I believe the garden needs a little attention. Keeping the weeds down is something I never seem to have enough time for."

"I suppose I could help with that. Would this afternoon be okay?"

Selena smiled. "Now might be better. You shouldn't work plants when the sun is full. They tend to dry out."

"I see." Dani was observing her nearly as closely as she was eyeing him. "Do you think my clothes might be dry yet?"

Her smile grew wider. "They'll probably be dry about the time you finish in the garden. You wouldn't want to wear them out there anyway. They might get dirty and dusty again."

Dani finished his tea and stood up. "Very well. Could you show me where you keep your garden tools?"

Selena led him to the back door, and pointed to a small shed at the corner of the garden.

Dani stepped down to a stone path leading to the garden. In the shed he found a hoe. He walked carefully down the rows of plants, carefully pulling weeds loose with the hoe. At the end of the row, he glanced back toward the cottage and saw that Selena was still watching him.

With a small smile on his face, Dani continued up and down the rows, enjoying the warmth of the soil between his toes and the warm light on his skin.

Finishing up, Dani put the hoe away, and walked over to the clothesline. His clothes and Roni's were dry, but the towels were still damp at the edges. He gathered everything but the towels.

Wiping his feet as best he could, Dani took the clothes back in to the table in front of the couch, where he folded Roni's clothes for him. Then taking his own, he went back into the bathroom for another shower.

Selena had watched his every move, of course.

When Dani came out of the bathroom, Roni was sitting up, with the quilt gathered around his waist.

"Get dressed, Roni. We'll have breakfast in a minute or so."

Roni looked apprehensively over toward Selena.

Dani smiled. "She won't mind. Go ahead."

Roni reluctantly stood up and got dressed quickly, muttering something about needing a toothbrush.

Dani looked at Selena. She smiled and started making pancakes.

He approached her and leaned against the counter. "You said you don't get much company."

Selena nodded, not allowing herself to be distracted from her task. "Just being polite. Actually I don't get any company. The only ones I see are the medical personnel, and the ground attendants. The ground attendants wear suits that cover them completely. I can't tell if they are men or women. I'm not allowed to talk with them."

"What about the medical people?"

"They talk to me. They don't seem to want to listen, except for documenting my case."

"Your case? You have a medical condition?"

"Well, I have a condition, I'm not sure it's entirely medical. I don't think I'm supposed to talk about it. You don't look like someone with a security clearance."

"Ah. You're probably right, but it does answer some questions for me anyway. That's probably why we're stuck here with you. It may be another security issue."

Selena stared at him for a moment, and then filled a plate with pancakes and handed it to him. Dani took it over to Roni.

When he returned to stand by Selena, she glanced at him. "You think he'll eat all that?"

"I know he will." Dani moved closer to the girl, looking up at her with expressive eyes. "I have appetites for more substantive things."

Selena chuckled. "You do seem a little more forward than your friend. Are you a playground Lothario?"

"I don't think so. I've never tried it on a playground." Dani paused. "That sounds a little kinky."

Selena smiled, turning the pancakes. "So you are flirting with me. I wasn't sure."

Dani chanced a soft grin. "I seemed to have your interest. Are you really that alone here?"

Selena nodded. "I think that's the truth. Before I ended up here, the boys I saw didn't look too different from what you and your friend do. I missed watching them grow up." She bit her lip.

"I guess it's okay to talk about boys and stuff." She relaxed a little. "What are they going to do, lock me up?"

"Not for anything you and I might get into, I'm sure." Dani responded. "I know you'd never ask me to do anything the least bit awkward." He smiled innocently at her.

"You *are* flirting with me! Okay, now I'm sure." Selena handed him a plate full of pancakes too. "You'd better eat up. I have a feeling you're going to be busy today."

Dani walked back to the table, looking over his shoulder at one point to see if she was watching him.

Selena turned back to her griddle and prepared her own breakfast. "Boys!" she thought, and then smiled.

Presently, she joined them at the table. "So what's on the agenda today, boys? More exploring?"

"I think I've had enough exploring for a while," Roni said. "I'd be happy to take another nap, and then eat some more." He paused, "I'm usually not this hungry."

"It's the great outdoors. It gives you a hearty appetite." Dani said. "Maybe I could go for another walk. Selena, would you like to show me around?"

"We could gather some apples, and peaches." Selena said. "Maybe later we'll bake some pies."

"That sounds like fun!" Dani enthused. "I'll help you make the pies."

"I'll help you eat the pies." Roni volunteered.

"That will be fine, Roni. You should rest up." Dani suggested. "I think I'd like walking through Paradise with a beautiful lady."

Selena stared at him. Roni just rolled his eyes.

20

May I kiss you?

"Do you have a favorite place?" Dani asked as they began their hike directly away from the garden.

"There are a couple of places where you can see across the valley. There's even ..." Selena hesitated, "There's even a small cave. It might be fun to build a fire there and camp out through the rain."

"I'd like that," Dani said softly, "but remember we have to make some pies for Roni. I'd like to do that another day maybe. It would be fun to snuggle around a campfire with you."

Selena stopped them, placing Dani on a slight elevation in front of her on the path. "It would be fun to snuggle around you, with a campfire nearby." She moved closer to him.

Dani looked up. Selena's normally fierce gaze was softened by a slight moistness in her eyes. He placed his hands on her cheeks and held her face steady. "You are very lovely, Selena. May I kiss you?"

"Please," Selena said softly, "Please kiss me."

Dani kissed her, holding the embrace for a long moment. Even their tongues found each other in a brief interlude.

"My ..." Selena said with a catch, "My first kiss." She leaned her head on his shoulder. "Thank you." She said with a whisper.

Selena wrapped her arms around him, letting her hands slide up under his polo shirt to tenderly hold his warmth against her. Dani placed his hands on the back of her shoulders.

"Oh, I wanted to touch you this morning. I wanted to rub my hands on you and play with you like a puppy." Selena said with a slight hoarseness to her voice. "I know you're just … I know you're too young to … oh, I don't know what I'm saying. I've been alone too long."

Dani could feel her tears dampening his shoulder.

"I'm not too young, Selena. There might be other reasons we should control ourselves, but my age is not one of them."

She continued rubbing her hands across the skin of his back, bringing them around to his ribs in a large circle.

"I would have let you touch me this morning. I would have been willing to lie on your kitchen table and let you rub your hands on me and play with me. I have played games like that with my sister. She would rub me, and I would rub her, and we both enjoyed it a lot."

He kissed her again. "I'm not too young."

She pulled back, with tears in her eyes. "But you must be! You're only a child, and I … oh I know this is wrong!"

"Selena," Dani lifted her face. "This is not wrong. Putting you in this place, and letting you grow up alone and try to figure things out by yourself; that's wrong. You're a lovely girl who needs to go out on dates, and go dancing, and go to parties. You need to meet people and find people who can look in your eyes with a goofy grin on their face and kiss you the wrong way until they figure out the right way. But this isn't wrong. I care for you, Selena. I'm not going to say I love you, because you're not ready to believe it, but I care for you as much as anyone could after knowing you for only a few hours. Let us be friends, Selena. Let us be good friends, and we will play games together not because they are wrong or right, but because they are fun, and we are friends."

Selena stared at him, and then she kissed him again, leaning him over and supporting his back, while her right hand rubbed over his belly and ribs. The tears, and the bright intensity of her eyes were one.

"You have moved from 'first kiss' to 'passion' with remarkable speed, young lady, but if we don't get back to your cottage and bake some pies, my friend Roni will be out in the forest gnawing on the tree bark to assuage his hunger." Dani said calmly.

Selena laughed, and helped them both to straighten up. "You aren't too young." She admitted. "You may look it, but you don't talk it. I may eventually end up with you on my kitchen table, but right now we have to make some pies."

21

She doesn't look that strong

Selena was remarkably adept at making pies. "I've practiced this relentlessly for several years. It's almost second nature to me now."

"You get around in the kitchen very well. I'm surprised you made the effort, since you have no one to cook for."

"I guess I was thinking, Dani, that if I ever *wanted* to have someone to cook for, I'd better know how to cook!"

"That's a remarkably logical way to look at it."

"My early training here was just basic household skills. Since I had to be here by myself, my trainers, all housewife types, made sure I knew how to take care of myself." She looked around. "Pretty soon, I had the garden, and then they set me up with a computer workstation so I could learn all the other stuff I needed."

Dani blinked. "Computer workstation?"

Selena smiled ruefully. "It's not what you think. Yes it's a computer, but it doesn't connect to anything but the Medical Department. I have to ask them the questions, and then they feed me the data."

"Oh." Dani replied, his disappointment evident.

"It's not as bad as it sounds." Selena looked into his eyes intensely, "They answered *all* of my questions, in painfully excruciating detail. I know, for instance," she wriggled her eyebrows, "*everything* there is to know about anatomy."

"That should be convenient," Dani said with more confidence than he felt.

"Indeed." Selena said, looking intently toward his shorts.

Dani had the feeling that she was remembering in distinct detail what the not-very-thick cloth concealed. He felt as though she were using X-ray vision on him.

"They also provided a rather extensive library. Your friend Roni has been working his way through it at a prodigious pace."

Dani looked over toward the small table in front of the couch. A collection of about eight books sat on it, neatly divided into a stack of three and another of five.

"I'm broadening my horizons," Roni mumbled.

o-o-o-o-o

Dani was sitting on Selena's back step, relaxing through a simulated "sunset" and its associated brief "twilight".

In her world, the Sun was a track of brilliant lights in an arc overhead, a football shape of about twenty powerful lights.

To simulate a sunset or sunrise, the shape was gradually powered up and advanced through the heavens by lighting more lamps along its path and allowing the ones behind to fade away. Although the track could be seen if you looked for it, it was also easy to ignore it and accept that the brilliant illumination came from the sun.

Somebody had a big power bill. Dani had also noted the strange mechanism of the four-o'clock rain. It was a simple irrigation device, arranged at the top of the curving canopy of sky and stars, which revolved around an ellipse to insure that all areas received their proper rainfall. It was just ordinary water, but probably treated with ozone. It had smelled like rain.

It provided a remarkable illusion, and kept the valley well stocked with growing things.

"Got a minute, Boss?" the voice of White Fang asked softly. Dani closed his eyes and leaned his head back against the wall.

"Go ahead." He responded silently.

"I have a preliminary report on the Selena saliva you obtained for us. It confirms that her DNA has been altered to reflect avian inclusions in certain areas."

"I obtained saliva?" Dani asked, puzzled.

"Yes. It was a masterful accomplishment, which prompted me to consider revising your status as agent to a double-O category. James Bond could not have done better."

"Oh. You're talking about Selena and I kissing. How nice that you were able to appreciate that." Dani mentally responded with wasted irony.

"Yes. I don't have any comments on style or technique, but the information collected was first-rate. Based only on where the avian inclusions were established in Selena's genome, I would predict that she has the ability to grow feathers, extend her arms to an impressive degree, and even modify her hands and feet into gripping talons."

Dani was tempted to open his eyes wide at this announcement. With some restraint, he managed to hold still. "You're saying she can fly?"

"That seems to be the purpose. We could confirm some of my suspicions if you would arrange to pick her up. Knowing her weight in comparison to her body's dimensions will tell us whether she might be able to get off the ground after transforming."

"Transforming?" Dani said with a mental gulp, "Into *what?*"

"Probably into something resembling a condor or large eagle. It wouldn't do to have something that could fly but would look too much like a human wearing a hang-glider." White Fang continued his dispassionate analysis.

"That would take a lot of strength. She doesn't look that strong." Dani said mentally.

"You don't look very strong, either, Your Puniness."

Dani considered. "So you're saying that Selena has been given some kind of MIL-SPEC-AP also."

"No. This is different. I would have recognized MIL-SPEC. This is heavier on the genetic blending, where MIL-SPEC emphasizes nanobots and programming."

"Before I was introduced to you, or you to me, Dad spoke to Mister

Jennison about a "Crow" Project." Dani shook his head. "But that was current or future work, Selena had to have started years ago."

"Maybe they are going to do a MIL-SPEC on an already existing genetic project." White Fang suggested.

"Maybe they need to." Mused Dani.

"We would have to see whether the current Selena meets the design parameters or not, to determine whether the unit might need to be further augmented." White Fang responded.

"I don't think she trusts us yet." Dani attempted to calm himself. "Speaking of augmentation, how's our new inductee?"

"The Roni Project is on schedule. The quad-core metabionic tanglenet system and its associated memory base are complete. The next step will be to establish a linkage and perform the download of the full MIL-SPEC-AP."

"Has Roni heard a voice in his head yet?"

"That would not be the procedure. The Roni will hear a synthesized personality only after the download is functional. You could establish a voice channel through the quad-core metabionic tanglenet system anytime you wish to begin."

"Wait, what? Are you saying I can talk to Roni through a mental link?" Dani almost sat bolt upright again.

"Yes, certainly. The Roni unit will be under your communications protocol."

"Let's take a walk." Dani said, getting up and heading back inside.

Roni was sitting in one of the comfortable chairs situated under a reading light.

"Hey, Roni, got a minute?" Dani approached him.

Roni looked up. "What's up?"

"I just wanted to talk to you. Can we take a walk?"

Roni looked out the window. "It's pretty dark out there."

"I'll help you," Dani held out his hand.

Roni set his book aside and took Dani's hand, letting himself be lifted and directed to the front door.

They stepped down onto the path and headed toward the gate.

"How can you see anything? All I see is those fake stars up there."

Dani looked over at his friend. His pupils were expanding, but clearly he had not dark-adapted yet.

"That's what you get for sitting under a lamp. Give it a few minutes." He led the boy back toward the wooden bridge.

In a few minutes, Dani directed Roni's hand to the handrail of the bridge, and stopped to look and listen as the water gurgled below.

"I need to talk with you, about your upgrade."

"Is that what allows you to see in the dark?" Roni asked.

"I guess." Dani looked around. "I think it's time to begin the next phase of your MIL-SPEC-AP. Your built-in computer system should be complete by now. I'm supposed to be able to send you signals from my computer to yours."

"Signals?"

"White Fang, give me a channel to Roni. I want to speak to him." Dani commanded mentally.

"Just think your words at him the same way that you think them to me. It's ready."

"Roni, this is Dani," Dani said mentally, "speaking to you through our computer linkage. Can you hear me?"

"I hear you," Roni's eyes got big, as he looked over to Dani. "How are you doing that?"

"No, no. You have to answer silently." Dani sent again, "Try it again by just thinking the words at me."

"That's impossible," Roni responded, but his lips had not moved. "Isn't it?"

"Not for us," Dani grinned, "We're secret agents, and this is one of our secrets!"

"Oh, man! I can't believe it!"

"We're just getting started! Next I have to send the MIL-SPEC download into your computer so that your nanobots will get the information needed to complete your upgrade. Are you ready?"

"Sure! What do I have to do?"

"Hang on." "White Fang, send the MIL-SPEC-AP upgrade information developed for the Roni Unit, and implement all the procedures just as was done for me."

"Initiating." White Fang answered.

"Okay, Roni, it's starting."

"I can't tell anything is happening, except that it sounds like the water down there is making more noise."

"I guess we'd better get you back into the house. You'll probably want to eat and sleep even more for a while." Dani took his friend's hand once more and they turned back toward the cottage.

"The next thing that will happen is that your new program specs will start talking to you. You will hear a voice telling you how to train for and operate your new abilities. But I don't know how long it will take before that voice wakes up. We'd better get you settled down."

"A voice in my head?" Roni said, *"Another* voice?"

"Yeah. I call my voice White Fang. How about if we call your voice Captain Obvious? We're sort of a military organization now, aren't we?"

"Captain Obvious? I guess it will be pretty obvious to me who's talking inside my head, so yeah, I guess that's okay."

"Okay, I'll set it up then. Hang on." "White Fang, set up the MIL-SPEC-AP program to use the name Captain Obvious when speaking to the Roni Unit."

"Yes, Sir!" came the response.

"All right, Roni. It's all set. In a few days, if we walk out like this again, we won't need to hold hands."

Roni hesitated. They stopped.

"Dani," Roni said softly, using his voice, "I ... I don't mind holding hands with you and walking in the darkness. I trust you, and ... and I like you."

Dani suspected what was coming. "It's all right, Roni." He said, taking both hands in his own. "I like you too." He kissed the other boy softly. "We'll still be friends. We'll be inseparable friends!" He kissed him again, "But I have to warn you, I still like kissing girls better!"

"No wonder! You get to kiss all the girls! Have you kissed Selena yet?"

"Um, yeah, we kissed. But I'm not supposed to tell about things like that. I don't want to 'kiss and tell', you know."

"It's all right. I'll keep your secret. I suspected you had. She can't seem to keep her eyes off of you."

"Heh. She was doing that before. She doesn't mind looking at you, either. I think she missed flirting with boys because she was growing up alone here."

"Oh, I hadn't thought about that."

"Maybe you could try being a little more friendly with her. Ask her tomorrow if maybe she has some chores for you to do to help her, especially if they are any really dirty chores, where she has to watch you to make sure you do it right."

"Really?"

"Oh yeah! Tell her I suggested it."

Spontaneously, Roni grabbed Dani and hugged him. "It's good to have a friend!"

"Oh, certainly! How else could we get into so much trouble?" Dani grinned. In the darkness, Roni could not see it. They continued on to the house.

22

I look kinda skinny

(Thursday, Oct 17, 2142)
Timeline: _____|_____

Dani and Roni both found themselves volunteered for something Selena was calling "Spring Cleaning".

Roni, as Dani had anticipated, was naked in the back yard, beating a rag rug from the living room, under Selena's piercingly direct supervision. Long after the rug had surrendered its last grains of sand, or they had been beaten to powder and the rug had surrendered its dust, Selena had Roni switching to the other side to smack futilely on it because as Selena had said, "The light is better there."

Meanwhile, Dani was tasked with moving all the light furniture out of the way to conduct a very thorough sweeping. He also was performing his duties in the nude because, Selena said, "You will get your clothes dirty too." This despite the fact that she already had both his and Roni's clothes in the washing machine.

While Dani was allowed to work unsupervised, he did collect an occasional affectionate pat on the rump for his diligence as Selena was passing by. Apparently his coaxing Roni into doing chores met entirely with her approval.

Finally, Selena allowed her crew to bring the rug back in and position it. The small furniture was brought back in also.

"All right, that should do it then. One more item on the cleanup list to take care of." She picked up her drawing tablet and a couple of towels and shooed the boys out toward the pond.

At last the purpose of the diving board was proven. Thankful to get the stinky dust off of them at last, Dani and Roni dove and splashed in the clear water of the pond.

Selena sat quietly on a low rock wall and sketched them.

Presently Dani approached her, evaluating the current drawing. Roni followed him, his former bashfulness apparently forgotten after the day's immersive lesson in naturism.

"That looks good. Any drawing in which I can recognize myself is a lot better than I can do."

"I look kinda skinny." Roni said.

"You are kinda skinny," Selena responded. "But I still appreciate your being models for me."

"And working our tails off for you." Roni said.

"Not completely," Selena responded, holding up another sketch, showing him diving in with a nice form.

"You're very talented. It's hard to capture a form in motion like that." Dani said.

"So you're agreeing with me that Roni has a nice butt, right?"

"I'm just saying that's an accurate portrayal." Dani stammered.

"Good, because you have a cute butt too." She held up another sketch. Roni looked it over and compared the two.

"She's got you there, Dani."

"At least it's a back view."

"Oh, we can fix that. How about taking up a pose on the diving board for just a minute? Then we'll head home."

Roni ran and jumped back in from the shore. Dani worked his way around and walked out to stand at the end of the board, hands raised in preparation. After a few minutes, he dove in and swam back to where Selena was watching. She finished up a few quick strokes and gestured toward the towels.

Dani and Roni began toweling themselves dry while Selena packed up her art materials. They all set off back to the cottage; Roni trying to keep his towel wrapped around himself while Dani merely draped his across his shoulders.

"Stay here a minute, boys. I have something for you." Selena went into her bedroom with her drawings.

She came back out in a moment to sit at the table with a small stack of clothing.

"Since you boys have no clothes other than the ones on the line, I thought you might consider wearing these, which are too small for me anyway." She held up a pair of panties. They didn't have lace ruffles, but the ones she was holding were pink.

She also had some blue, green, and other colors.

"You want us to wear panties?" Roni sputtered.

"Hey at least it's not thong underwear!" Selena responded.

"Thong underwear?" Dani said speculatively. "Do you have it in leather?"

Roni looked at him aghast, but Selena merely grabbed him and hugged him. She rubbed his back and his buttocks, and then turned him around. "Here," she commanded, "just step into these. Let's see how they look."

Dani allowed her to continue her game of embarrassment. He stepped into the garment and Selena pulled it up around his waist. He looked down. "It's almost the same color as me. It looks like I'm not wearing anything."

"The alternative," Selena pointed out, "is to not wear anything."

Dani turned in place, letting the others see what it looked like.

"It's almost worse than not wearing anything," Roni said. "The eye is drawn to your ... package."

"My package wouldn't fill up a watch-pocket," Dani said, looking down. "Oh, I see what you mean." The smooth fabric was pushed out as if he had a pinecone under a tablecloth.

"It looks fine," Selena said. "Here, Roni, you try it, or do I have to dress you as well?" She handed him the blue pair.

Roni put them on. He had the same problem as Dani. At least

neither of the boys had an erection. What they did have though, was apparent.

"I think it would be better to wear a breechcloth, like maybe a dishtowel and a belt." Dani suggested.

"Don't be ridiculous!" Selena said sternly, "We're not using dish towels as underwear. You'll just have to adjust. No sense letting good clothes go to waste when you have nothing else to wear."

"Would it really bother you if we decided not to wear anything?" Dani asked. Roni looked at him and slowly nodded.

"You know, I have some old sundresses that are too small for me too. Now where did I pack them up?" Selena looked around. "It's kinda fun dressing you up, you know."

"Never mind. No dresses, please." Roni begged.

Dani watched him, and shrugged his shoulders.

"Now, boys, let's put together some dinner!" Selena said.

Dani realized that the matter was settled, and he would be wearing her outgrown panties for the foreseeable future. Selena was making up for not having been exposed to social situations. She had become quite the manipulator.

He went out to the clothesline, wearing his pink panties, and noticed that the clothes were completely dry. However, realistically, they wouldn't be able to wear the same clothes all the time. He brought in the clothes and folded them.

Roni was setting the table. Dani strove not to look at him as he paraded around in girl's underwear. Then he adjusted his own panties and sat down. His eyes were drawn to a chalkboard near the refrigerator. On it, under the words "tea" and "sugar", was written "leather thong underwear for Dani".

He looked toward the opposite wall. In the molding work between the ceiling and wall, a beady lens was apparent. A camera focused on the kitchen.

He and Roni were obviously known to be prisoners here, and Selena was so used to being watched that she assumed it was a convenience. His mind returned to their predicament along with a soft indrawn breath.

Knowing now what they looked like, Dani spotted numerous other camera positions. Basically anywhere within the house, and for most areas visible near it, everything they did was observable to the hidden watchers. They had as much privacy in this dwelling as they had under Selena's chore management.

"White Fang," Dani addressed his inner agent silently, "can you give me an assessment of Roni's progress, without alerting him to your interest?"

"I can simply interrogate his monitor, if that's what you mean. He is progressing well. His vision has been modified; his senses enhanced, and his muscles and skeleton are being strengthened."

"Is it too late to make him a little stronger? He thinks he looks skinny, and I think he'd like to look a little healthier."

"I think you both need to look a little healthier, but he is in the middle of his upgrades. It would be 'child's play' to further enhance his musculature."

"Funny. Make sure you don't carry it too far. I like to think I have a swimmer's physique. I think Roni would like to appear more like a ballplayer."

"Bigger shoulders and arms, chest, and more muscular legs? Is that what you had in mind?"

"Yes, but nothing out of proportion. I want him to be pleasantly surprised, not driven crazy."

"I think I know what you have in mind. I'll upgrade the upgrade. You realize he's going to be even hungrier now?"

"Is he getting enough? I've noticed that our diet consists primarily of fruits and vegetables. Should we get more protein?" Dani eyed the shopping list again.

"The Roni Project is getting more than enough energy. We'll keep his energy budget within normal parameters, or we may just suggest to him that he supplement his diet inside the house with some foraging forays outside."

"How much longer until he's fully equipped?" Dani asked silently.

"Two more days should suffice. But that's only his base level upgrade. He will be putting on mass for another two weeks. He still needs to go through extensive training in how to use the changes. So do you for that matter."

"I understand, but we can't do much while being under constant observation. I know that much about operational security."

"Good. I'll stand ready, along with Captain Obvious, for the time you'll need to access your enhancements."

"Thanks. What's your assessment of how he's coping with all this?"

"The Roni Program is nominally on track to be a successful implementation of the MIL-SPEC-AP. The individual in question has been through a lot in his previous activities. It was not the kind of training I would have recommended, but it was very extensive. This portion of his MIL activities should be like a walk in the park."

"Thanks, White Fang, I appreciate your wording it that way. Your humor is a balm to my spirit." Dani responded with a smile.

"I'll try to cut back on any overly unmilitary behavior, Sir."

"Don't change on my part, White Fang. I like you just the way you are."

"Changes on your parts will be up to you, Sir. I plan to have nothing to do with that portion of your anatomy. White Fang out."

Dani smiled again, serendipitously as his food arrived in front of him. He and Roni ate with great appetites. It had been a most intriguing day!

23

Try to pick up a chick

(Friday, Oct 18, 2142)
Timeline: _____|_____

Dani awakened in the middle of the night. He looked over to Selena's bedroom door, only to see it closed. He had never seen it closed before.

Slipping out from his warm nest on the couch, Dani went over to Selena's door. It was locked from the inside. He had never investigated her bedroom before, considering it a violation of her privacy. Inwardly he chuckled at that.

But it occurred to him at this very late moment that the architecture of this cottage indicated that the loft area on this side of the house would be only accessible from inside Selena's bedroom. She must have a stairway to the loft.

Dani went out the front door as quietly as he could, closing it behind him. Although Selena's bedroom door was locked, her front door didn't even have a lock. He had never noticed that before.

Dani went around to the side of the house where Selena's loft would be visible. French doors led to a small parapet. The doors were open. That would be a good way to have ventilation in her bedroom suite, but Dani had a feeling something else was going on.

He walked over to the bushes that defined the side of the yard, and concealed himself among them to watch for a while.

Above him, the simulated stars appeared to twinkle, but he realized after observing them steadily that he was seeing random fluctuations in their power supply, intended to seem like twinkling. The repetition was entirely too steady, if you concentrated on a single "star".

None of this surprised him. The effort to reproduce the standard constellations did, however. Dani realized that he was looking at a permanent display of the North American Hemisphere in mid-winter. The colors were off, but the placement was accurate.

Studying the stars like this, Dani realized he was seeing a shadow obscuring them at intervals. This chamber was so large that only one star out of a dozen would be blocked at a time by something up nearly against the roof of the cavern. Something small for the distance.

Something approximately human-sized.

Selena.

Dani continued watching, finally understanding the slow circling route she was taking up in her own vault of the heavens. Selena was flying, coasting along under her own power nearly two hundred feet in the air.

Dani enhanced his vision as much as possible, but he could still only see an occasional silhouette. Whatever her form consisted of, it was likely entirely dark. He thought he would like to see her more closely, but realized after a moment's thought that it would probably be rather nightmarish.

If her arms had become wings, and her feet talons, then it could be assumed that the rest of her would look like a bird. He had kissed her lips. Would her face now have a beak like an eagle?

She operated under a strict personal security protocol. She wouldn't like being discovered, being seen in her secret form.

Suddenly Dani decided that he didn't want to see her in her transformed state, and that he especially didn't want her to see *him*. Making sure that she was still circling around up at the top of her realm, he made his way back to the porch and went back inside.

He wondered whether her transformation might be painful for her.

He wondered whether she could see well enough in the dark to have spotted him lurking down in her yard wearing her old underwear. He wondered what it might be like to kiss an eagle's beak. He wandered into dreamland and fell asleep.

o-o-o-o-o

The next morning, his third day in Selena's World, Dani awoke rather early feeling unusually refreshed. Keeping his eyes closed, he called up White Fang.

"I feel really good. What's going on?"

"Why shouldn't you feel good?"

"Well I don't *mind* feeling good, but I usually have to work up to it. This feels different. It's better, but it's different."

"As your MIL-SPEC-AP agent, I don't have a lot of control over what you choose to do in meeting your obligations. When I decide that you've been doing a good job, I like to reward you for your effort. All I have to do is tweak your endorphins and then you wake up with a smile on your face. Militarily, that's a positive start no matter what you have to face."

"Huh. I didn't know that. What happens if I don't do a good job?"

"I'd give you a scolding before you went to sleep. But I still have to keep you in top shape, so you'll still feel okay. You'll just have to get used to feeling good."

"I'll look forward to it. What should I do today to be able to wake up tomorrow feeling really good?"

"Exercise, proper diet, try to pick up a chick, that sort of thing."

"Pick up a chick? What do you mean by that?"

"Remember we wanted to estimate Selena's weight? If you can pick her up, we can get a reading and calculate her body mass. That will give us a strength requirement for her ability to fly."

"Well, we know she can fly. I saw her last night."

"You did what? Where was I?" White Fang responded.

"You were with me, of course. Well, let me say I didn't really see her fly, I just saw an occasional silhouette and I assumed it was hers." Dani explained.

"Assumptions aren't evidence, but in this case, it could hardly be anything else. Can you replay what you observed for me?"

"How can I do that? It was last night."

"Just think about what you saw. Try to visualize it in as much detail as you can. You aren't limited to speech alone, you know."

Dani concentrated on what he remembered about seeing the stars, the way they twinkled, and the way they were temporarily obscured by something. In a minute, he seemed to have gotten the message across. "Did you get it?" he asked mentally.

"I got your image sequence. Good deduction, Sir! You should get a gold star for that report."

"Thanks." Dani responded with a droll attitude. "But what did you mean about I'm not limited to speech alone?"

"Any message on a tanglenet system can be transmitted to any other part of the system." White Fang recited as if reading from a manual.

"But what does that mean? How many parts of the system can I reach, and what can I send?" Dani asked in genuine puzzlement.

"Currently there are four nodes on your existing tanglenet system; yourself, White Fang, Captain Obvious, and the Roni Unit. You can send voice messages, visual impressions, smells, tastes, and manual operation instructions as well as receive the feedback from manual operations."

"Let's go over that last part again. I can send manual operation instructions to whom?"

"White Fang and Captain Obvious don't have hands to be operated, but you can send manual operating instructions to the Roni Unit. You can make his hands do things, and feel what they are doing. You can make his legs walk, and you can see through his eyes."

"No way! I don't believe you!" Dani was astonished.

"Truth. You would require his cooperation to be the receiving unit, or to be unconscious, but it will work for you. You can also let him control your hands or legs if you want him to."

"And he can see through my eyes?" Dani blinked mentally.

"You can both see through the other's eyes, once you practice what your new abilities give you."

"Wow! I told him we would be inseparable, but this goes way beyond anything I thought it would."

"There aren't many limits. Anything in your nervous system can be transmitted to the other node."

"What about you? If I were hurt or injured; let's say I was rendered unconscious, could you walk me out of danger?"

"I suppose it's theoretically possible. It's not a part of my training or my program."

"But if we practiced it?" Dani persisted.

"It should be possible." White Fang conceded.

"Okay, the next time I'm stuck doing something that's crushingly boring, I may just turn it over to you to complete."

"There may be a learning curve involved." White Fang suggested.

"Try to keep up, then. Practice along with me when I'm learning something new, or doing something dangerous. If I get injured, you may be my only rescuer, and if something fatal happens to me, you'll be out of the picture too."

"Message received, Sir."

"Cool! You don't know how to play the piano, do you?"

"Based on the musical skills you already have, it shouldn't take long to pick up. We'll need access to a piano." White Fang seemed almost enthusiastic.

"I can't lay here any more. I'm too excited, and I feel great too."

"Have a nice day, Sir." White Fang replied with his own version of droll.

24

How can you not do that?

Dani opened his eyes and sat up. Selena was at the kitchen table already with her tea. Dani smiled at her.

Selena got up to get him his own cup of tea.

Dani got up and stretched. "I feel good today!" he said to Selena.

She glanced at his torso. He was still wearing the panties. "Should I take these off now?" He teased her.

"Suit yourself," she smiled.

Dani approached the table and sat down. "You can get used to almost anything, I guess. These felt pretty weird to wear at first."

"You did look a little strange, I have to admit. I suppose I can get used to things too."

"But you didn't want to get used to seeing me entirely naked, I guess."

Selena pushed his tea forward again. "I wouldn't mind, but I also wanted to practice what they call 'the social niceties', and wearing clothes of some sort is at least a part of that."

"I'll have to remember that. I tend to forget it from time to time."

"You seem surprisingly comfortable to be naked."

"It depends on the circumstances. Sometimes it seems the most natural thing in the world. Where we come from, the public pools for children don't require bathing suits. Kids get used to it really quickly."

"That does sound like fun."

Dani shrugged. "Among other things, it means there's no barrier of extra cost to anyone. And the differences among children of that age seem totally unimportant. The rules for teenagers are somewhat more restrictive. That's one of the reasons I decided not to become one."

Selena seemed to have some trouble with her drink. "What was that? You decided not to become a teenager? How can you do that? Or how can you *not* do that?"

"My dad works pretty high up in Genano. He was able to get all of us into a program where our age was frozen at a particular stage. We don't get older anymore."

"Well, that's convenient, I suppose. So what were the other reasons you didn't want to become a teenager? You look to be what, about ten?"

"Pretty much ten precisely. I saw a lot of other kids in my condo and in the parks around it. When they started stretching out and growing taller and gangly, with hair on their faces and all that, I just thought they were losing everything that makes childhood wonderful. It seemed to me that they were turning into something between a werewolf and a zombie."

Dani sipped on his tea, and looked up again. "I liked playing baseball, riding my bike, and going swimming with the other kids. I knew all that would have to change if I became a teenager. It scared me out of my wits, but I didn't know what I could do about it."

He drank again. "I would have to wear ugly clothes, get a bigger bicycle, and I wouldn't be able to play the kind of games we did at the swimming pool. The teenagers can't even *touch* each other." He blinked. "Then my dad came home one day and said they had found a way to freeze people at their current age. He wanted to go into the program, just mom and him, so that they could remain relatively young adults, and he could stay with the company and the work that he loved for as long as possible."

He smiled. "Mom got a little upset when he said it would be just them. She wanted me to go into the program too. I guess we had a kind of special relationship. Still do, I suppose. She thinks of me almost like a baby, her baby boy. She knew I loved being a kid, and that it would bother me even more than her to have to become a teenager. Dad was kinda worried that if I didn't grow up anymore, he would never have grandchildren, I guess."

Dani paused in thought. "No, it was more than that. I think he was worried that I would never become an adult; that I would never take responsibility or be worth anything, and that it would be his fault."

Selena merely waited quietly.

"So they asked me. I knew how Mom felt, of course. I knew it would make her deliriously happy to be able to keep her little boy, and I wanted that too! I liked being loved, and Mom does it better than anyone. So I said oh please oh please yes, let me be this age forever! Mom was excited, and I was happy, but then I saw Dad, and he looked worried. I thought at the time that he was concerned about something technical in the process. But it was actually something else; he was worried that I would be spoiled somehow, and never reach my true potential, probably blaming him for doing it to me."

Dani looked up. There were tears in his eyes. "I didn't find out about that until long after. But Dad came around eventually. I don't think he worries about that anymore, and that pleased me when it happened. Anyway, they scheduled the procedures. I was probably the youngest ever to undergo it at Genano, and I became permanently ten years old." He sat back and became quiet.

"So that's why you're not really ten years old then. You do seem more mature than just ten."

"Oh, no, I'm really ten in every way you can measure. That hasn't changed at all. The maturity or seeming maturity just comes from having been ten for a long time."

"Being ten for a long time," Selena rolled the words around in wonder. She stared at him. "Dani, how long ago *was* this? How old *are* you?"

Dani smiled at her. "I just squeaked in at the end of the last century. My next birthday, I could have forty-three candles on my birthday cake, but I always insist on just ten."

Selena's eyes grew huge. She stared at him, and then began looking at his entire body once again, trying to reconcile what her mind was trying to encompass against what her eyes were telling her.

"I can't believe it," she said breathlessly.

"I know," Dani said ruefully, "I try not to tell people about it, but it tends to slip out." He looked down. "Some people don't take it well."

"I'm sorry." Selena shook her head. "I don't mean to be insulting."

"You're not. You've been wonderful. You treat me as a friend, and that's all I ask of life. I like having friends."

"And your parents?"

"They're still very young at heart. Dad still works at Genano, and Mom still gives me a bath when I visit there." He smiled. "She knows, of course, but it's just more fun to pretend, and it's a game we both play."

"It seems like a game you play with everyone you meet."

"No, I'm really ten years old with everyone I meet, until it's time to be more than that if I want to. But I don't allow just anyone to give me a bath. Only my friends."

"I didn't give you a bath," Selena said, "Yet."

"No, but you made me take a shower, and stole my clothes, and ogled me like I was the ripest berry you had ever seen."

"Yes, I did all that." She admitted.

"So basically, you treated me as a friend."

"You really think that?"

He nodded. "And you owe me a bath."

"What?" She exclaimed.

"I want you to give me a bath. I told you that I like being ten years old, and that I like it when my mother treats me like her baby boy. I like having women give me a bath."

"You are more twisted than I could have imagined." Selena shook her head and stared at him.

"And you made me take my clothes off, and then you dressed me in your panties." Dani stood up. "What kind of games were you playing?"

"Oh, I'm sorry. I should have been more respectful."

"Not at all. You were perfect. You were playing the games I love to play, even when you didn't know we were playing a game."

"You must think I'm terrible."

"I think you're wonderful!" Dani came around the table, and placed his arms around her back and under her knees. Then he picked her up as if she were the baby. "Should I give you the bath instead?"

Selena laughed. "How are you doing that? You must be very strong."

Dani sat her back down again. "I try to go through life letting people underestimate me. Then when I do something, it seems all the more remarkable. Who would have expected that from a ten-year-old?"

Selena smiled. "All the more remarkable, yes indeed. Let me take you in and give you a bath." She took his hand, and led him into the bathroom.

Roni had looked up a minute or two before. Watching Selena lead Dani into the bathroom, he just lay back down and closed his eyes.

In the bathroom, Selena drew hot water into the tub. As it was filling, she removed the panties from Dani. Both were smiling.

Then Selena removed her own clothes, setting them aside to keep them dry. Naked, she turned back to the boy.

Dani was staring at her. He had fully expected that she would show signs of her secret avian capabilities, but all he saw was an exceptionally attractive and shapely sixteen-year-old girl

Selena helped him into the tub, and knelt down beside it. She took up a cloth and some soap, and she began bathing him as if he were an infant.

Dani relaxed, letting the process take place. It truly was a comfort to him. He idly reached out to caress her breast, finding it not only surprisingly pert and shapely, but also quite firm, verging on the muscular. He ran his hand along her ribcage, noting the same muscularity over her entire shape. While she had been remarkably light for him to pick up, she was also clearly very strong, with muscles that were quite firm even when she was relaxing.

Dani had the impression that she could easily bench press at least five times her own weight. And even that calculation assumed that her weight was normal for her size.

Selena's skin showed no indication of abnormality. It was flawless and somewhat dark in complexion. It would be wonderful to watch her transform into her other shape, but what he had right now was quite wonderful also. Dani relaxed again and let her hands bathe him, and lull him into a drowsy comfort zone.

He obeyed her softly whispered instructions without thought, simply moving as she instructed him.

Selena took the opportunity to investigate him entirely, and without embarrassment. He was a wonder, and she was enjoying the delight he represented.

She carefully laved the area between his legs, manipulating his miniature equipment tenderly and with puzzlement. She honestly believed that he was truly old enough to be middle-aged, but he showed no inclination at all of responding to her caresses. His miniature tool was not flaccid or shrunken; it was merely tiny, as if it had never been given the impetus or opportunity to grow.

He was, in every way, a mere ten-year-old boy, allowing her to caress him and play with him as if he were her own dolly. She washed away any sense of guilt or misgivings with the same cloth that she used to clean his soft and remarkably pliant skin.

Even his toes were tiny replicas of what she knew feet could display. He was small, and tender, and lovingly cute. She thought about drying him, and taking him into her own bed to fondle him until the darkness came again.

Reluctantly, she bade him stand, rinsing his body of soap and rubbing his skin with her bare hands. She raised his arms and stroked smoothly down from his upper arms across his armpit, devoid of hair, and then down across his ribs to his upper legs, and down over his knees to his calf muscles. It was all smooth unblemished skin, and a delight to caress.

Drying him, Selena used some of her own perfume on him, knowing that eventually she would be holding him and smelling it again, hopefully in her bed. She realized that she had become quite smitten with the boy.

Selena rationalized any thoughts of concern to the back of her mind. She was loving this boy as if he were her own child, her first lover, and her dream prince, come to rescue her.

Sighing, Selena finished her attention to the body in front of her, and

25

Have you enjoyed your visit?

(Friday, Oct 18, 2142)
Timeline: _____|_____

Roni woke up to the smell of breakfast. It was only slightly more intriguing than the smells emanating from Dani's body. He sniffed again; Dani smelled good, but he didn't smell like Dani. He was undoubtedly clean. There was no pond smell emanating from him. But he was adorned in Selena's perfume for some reason.

Roni kissed him, bringing him to wakefulness.

"Oh, it's you." Dani yawned. "I was having the nicest dream."

"If you were dreaming that Selena gave you a bath, it wasn't a dream. You still smell like a Marseilles cat-house."

Dani hugged Roni affectionately. "You'd better not let her hear you say that. This is her perfume."

"It's a nice perfume for her. It doesn't do much for you."

"It got you over here, didn't it?"

"I think maybe you were just a barrier on the way to the breakfast table."

"Hmm. I can smell it too. All right, if you'll get off of me, you lummox, I can get up too."

Roni kissed him again, and then climbed off him. Dani noticed that Roni was still wearing his blue panties. He looked down at himself. His were yellow.

The boys settled to the table. Selena had put on quite a spread. She had scrambled eggs and sausage, with biscuits and fresh milk. She came over and gave Dani a kiss directly on his lips. Then she moved over and presented the same to Roni.

"Whoa! What's that for?" Roni exclaimed.

"I like having handsome young gentlemen come to visit me occasionally." Selena said calmly.

"And we didn't even have to dance naked first." Roni said appreciatively.

"I'll do it," Dani chirped up, "but maybe later. This looks great!"

"I was hungry too. Eat up, boys. No doubt we'll find other mischief to get into later."

"Here's to mischief," Dani raised his glass, and was quickly joined in the toast.

"Dani is a great dancer." Roni said, "He and his sister took ballet lessons."

"Ballet? You?" Selena raised a dark eyebrow.

"It was Mom's idea. She liked dressing us up in fancy outfits." To Selena's curious look, he admitted, "Of course, I was being a little girl at the time."

Roni choked on his food. "You what?" Selena was looking at him curiously as well.

"When Lori was growing up, we had trouble finding baby-sitters. I volunteered to become a girl for a while so that I could be responsible for Lori. It worked great. She was four years old when we started, and we grew up as sisters together, sleeping together and dressing alike. Well, she grew up; I was ten years old all through it. Then when Lori turned eighteen, I started transitioning back to being a boy, but we continued sleeping together."

"I need a drink," Roni muttered, reaching for his milk glass.

"She was eighteen, and you were a ten-year-old boy, and you were sleeping together?" Selena confirmed.

Dani nodded. "We had a lot of fun."

142

Selena looked thoughtful. "Maybe I should let you sleep with me, or am I too young for you?"

Dani smiled. "We could have a lot of fun too."

"Well, I know that's going to happen," Roni proclaimed. "Don't forget to kiss me good-night, both of you. I'll just be keeping a lonely vigil out here."

"You're probably wondering," Selena said by way of diversion, "where the extra groceries came from. I made a long shopping list. I even arranged for you boys to have some new clothes"

She smiled. "And Dani, I got you the leather thong underwear you asked about."

Dani looked at her and smiled. "Cool! Would it be okay to wear that instead of being naked when I dance for you?"

Selena studied him. She swallowed, even though she hadn't had any food to swallow. "I would like that," she said very softly.

"If I only had a camera," Roni muttered, "I could make a lot of money." Dani smiled at him.

o-o-o

Selena had four sets of outerwear for them, and a half-dozen each of proper boy's briefs. Well, perhaps not too proper, these all had cartoon characters printed on them. Roni thought they were a great improvement over girl's underwear though, and he selected an outfit and headed off to take a bath.

Selena suggested that they move their sleeping quarters up to the reading room loft on the other side of the house from her bedroom. It was a cozy area with a long cushion and many small pillows under the wide windows.

The stairway to this loft had been concealed behind yet another bookcase. Dani carried the rest of their new clothes and their quilt up to the loft and found a shelf for himself and one for Roni.

Dani continued wearing the yellow panties, even after Roni had come out of the bathroom fully dressed.

Roni patted Dani's derriere affectionately a time or two while walking by him. Dani merely blew him a kiss.

Selena brought out the leather thong underwear to show the boys. Dani was admiring it and planning which musical piece he might use with it for entertaining Selena.

Roni said, "Hey, there's someone at the gate!"

Dani looked out the window. It was Rob Jennison.

"I'll be right back!" Dani ran up the stairs to the reading loft and changed clothes quickly, leaving the thong underwear and the yellow panties, and pulling on a new pair of underwear and a shorts and top outfit.

Coming back down the stairs, Dani saw Rob Jennison just coming in the front door.

"Hey, Mister Jennison! I'm surprised to see you here." Roni was greeting him.

"Good Morning, boys. Good Morning, Miss Selena. Thank you for entertaining these young men while we were trying to get things sorted out."

"You knew we were here?" Dani asked bluntly.

"We put you here." Jennison responded. "Have you enjoyed your visit?"

"We've had some fun." Dani persisted. "You realize that what you've done constitutes kidnapping."

"I hope that if I ever get locked up it will be in a place as nice as this!" Jennison continued deflecting. Dani realized that he was being a consummate politician, and that the next few minutes would be a significant negotiation.

"Please sit down, Mister Jennison," Selena said smoothly. "Would you care for some tea?"

"Thank you, I'd like that." Jennison took a seat comfortably. "Well, boys, I guess you'd like to know what this is all about, eh?"

Dani and Roni nodded to each other and each took a seat. "I would assume it has something to do with the MIL-SPEC-AP download I got when we were visiting Genano." Dani said forthrightly.

"Ah, yes, getting right to the point, I see." The man looked slightly uncomfortable. "We've been wondering how we could keep this under wraps somehow."

"Certainly a very private kidnapping is a way to keep things quiet." Dani continued.

"While technically accurate as a term, we all know that neither of you is anywhere near being a kid." Jennison said pleasantly. "Anyway, my agency is interested in making the best of a sticky situation. We'd like to work with you to try to find a way to justify your new-found skills."

"So it was accidental then, or something you hadn't anticipated." Dani sought to confirm.

"We hadn't anticipated it, that's for sure." Jennison admitted.

"Good, that confirms for me that I wasn't responsible for anything going wrong."

"How can you say that? Who else would have been responsible?"

Dani shrugged his thin shoulders. "Whoever set up the security on the program I guess. I just want it made clear that I was not engaged in espionage, or whatever the accusation might be."

"No one's being accused of anything." Jennison protested.

"Not true. You've been accused of kidnapping, and you're here for a reason."

"More tea, Mister Jennison?" Selena asked quietly.

"Thank you." Jennison sat still for a moment, letting Selena's distraction give him time to think.

"Can you tell me how it happened, at least?" Jennison pleaded.

"As you know, we were there to use the Genano imaging technology." Roni nodded. Dani continued, "My own cybernetic devices were trying to keep up, and eventually reported that the data stream was beyond their capacity. On a machine level request, I was asked if an upgrade would be permitted." Dani paused, "Actually, I was given three choices. I could suspend the display program offering, I could degrade the presentation format, or I could implement an upgrade which had a better chance of utilizing the data properly."

Rob nodded. "And you chose the upgrade."

"I did."

"Did you know it was a proprietary military application designed for the government by Genano?"

"I only knew that I was in Genano, that the offering had come from Genano, and that all of my previous capabilities had been developed by Genano. As far as I knew, this was merely one more in a series of programs for clients of Genano."

"Did you consult with your father about your decision?"

"Both my father and Mister Winthrope," Dani said, nodding toward Roni, "were present, but neither was a party to my machine-level negotiation. It was a matter between me, and whatever was inside my head, about what was going to end up inside my head."

Jennison ran his hand through his thinning hair. Dani was reminded that Rob was no older, and possibly younger, than himself. He chose not to mention that fact.

"I see," said Jennison. He stopped to drink his cooling tea.

"My Application Agent and I have discussed this situation," Dani volunteered. "I pointed out that using a boy as a secret agent was not a very well thought-out program, and that my becoming a special capabilities soldier was even more unlikely."

He took a sip of his own tea. "Add to that, we several have been planning, along with Malcolm Horowitz, to build and crew a new kind of rocket ship, one using fusion technology to take off from Earth and reach orbit without a booster stage. I'm presuming the notoriety of this proposed venture would make me even less of a candidate for potential spy missions."

Jennison stared at him. "Believe it or not, that is yet another factor that I failed to put together, and I was instrumental in getting you that Genano viewing room appointment."

Dani sat back. "Well then no wonder you haven't been able to figure it out. It's all your fault."

"I didn't set up the machine level protocols on MIL-SPEC, you know."

Dani shrugged. "They'll want to blame you anyway." He grinned at Jennison. "You've got about six months or longer to figure out how your space-boy spy is going to be able to be effective, and then your goose will be cooked. Do you have any ideas?"

Jennison slumped. "None at all. Even if you go on a world tour, getting you from the publicity box into the hidden chambers of whatever would be an impossible task."

"Is Selena a part of your program too?" Dani asked.

"What?" Jennison looked up. "What are you talking about?"

"Her." Dani pointed with his head, "This." He looked around. "How in the world did you justify this?"

Rob gritted his teeth. "I inherited this." He looked up cagily. "What makes you think Miss Selena has anything to do with any of my programs?"

"Like me, she has special abilities that no one knows about. Did you ever develop a program to use her capabilities?"

"No." He said rather bitterly, glancing at the girl. "She's not quite there yet."

"Why not make her a part of my team?" Dani asked innocently.

"Your team?" Jennison asked, "Do you have some ideas you've thought of? A way to make this work?"

"A way to make it work better, maybe. I still don't know what you think any of us could do, being dropped behind enemy lines or whatever, but she could be the perfect insertion and retrieval agent."

"No," Rob shook his head. "She doesn't have the strength for that. I've concluded she likely never will."

"Have you considered what a dose of MIL-SPEC_AP could do for her?" Dani looked over at Selena. She was in a very confused state.

Jennison glared at him. "You've got to be kidding! How can making her a super-soldier improve her special abilities?"

"MIL-SPEC-AP comes in two flavors. I don't even want to know what you do with the soldiers, but the secret agent protocol has a lot of upgrade flexibility. If we upgraded her with it, I think she might be able to insert or extract me, for example. I don't weigh too much."

"How much do you weigh?" Selena asked.

"Forty–two kilograms. It's been that for a long time."

Selena considered. "That's getting closer, Mister Jennison."

Rob looked at the two of them. "I can't believe I'm seriously considering this."

"Well, you are pretty desperate. If they locked you up, it wouldn't be in a place as nice as this." Dani grinned again.

"No." Jennison agreed. "There's also the matter of getting approval for her upgrade. I'm already being watched like a … oh crap! … watched like a hawk."

"You wrap us up under your authorization umbrella, and I'll take care of the details."

"You …" Jennison was stunned. "You'll what?"

"I'll take care of the MIL-SPEC-AP for Selena, and make sure she's upgraded for the specified insertion and extraction procedures. You take care of finding the appropriate missions for us and keep the agencies off our backs. We'll answer to no one but you. Your employer will have to trust and depend upon you, or write off untold millions in already spent funding."

Jennison looked around at faces that were either equally perplexed, or radiating a false confidence.

"I might," He said slowly, "I just might be able to convince a few people. If you can do what you say you can do, we might all come out of this smelling like …" he stopped, and leaned toward Dani, sniffing audibly, "smelling like whatever you've gotten into, Mister Corrigan."

Dani kept his eyes away from Selena. He looked back at Jennison. "Do we have a deal?"

"We have a deal, Mister Corrigan!"

"Excellent!" Dani gloated. "My first requirement will be a key to this place. While it will be better to be able to come and go, my second priority will be a road trip." He looked over at Selena. "We were interrupted on our way to see Malcolm. I'd like you to come along and meet him too."

Selena's eyes were bright. "And shopping?"

Dani looked at Jennison. "My third requirement will be an expense account and a salary. We have to go shopping."

"I suspect that you're going to make an excellent leader. I'll give you a number where you can contact me, and we'll set up some discrete ways that I can keep tabs on you."

"That won't be a problem, Mister Rob. We're going to be very much in the public eye. Be sure to select your missions with great care."

"All right. You can stay here as long as you want, and the ways out will be shown to you. Also, I'll contact your mother and father and send them your regards. I'll tell them you've met and been staying with a new friend, but that you're on your way to Malcolm's. That should be sufficient for them. You should contact both Malcolm and your other friends Alicia and Anastasia Winthrope. You've been out of touch a few days and they've been making inquiries."

"Thanks Rob. It should be fun working with you. Let me know if you have any trouble selling this weird situation. It's important to both of us. We'll make it work."

"I'm putting a lot of faith in you, Dani. I don't know how you're going to make it all work, but I have confidence that you will. Good Luck!" Rob Jennison made his good-byes.

26

Yes, I can fly

"Wow! We can finally leave here. That's a relief." Roni exclaimed. "Oh, I'm so excited! I haven't been out of my gilded cage in *years!*"

"Patience, little ones. We still have some preparation work to do. And don't forget, I said I would dance for you. I still want to do that." Dani reminded them.

"Now that you mention it, I'm looking forward to seeing that, actually." Roni turned to Selena. "I've seen him dance before, and it's worth seeing again."

"Thanks, Roni. Selena, you and I have another appointment too. We have to figure out how to keep the promises I made to Mister Jennison."

"Oh, yes." Selena looked at him, "What did you have in mind?"

"Well, first I have to get my MIL-SPEC-AP internal agent working on modifying your nanobots to reshape your genome, keeping in mind your special changing ability, which so far I've only speculated about. Was I right that you have the ability to fly?"

Selena looked a little crestfallen. "Yes, I can fly, but I have to change myself into a bird to do it."

"We are aware that you have bird DNA in your genome. Does it hurt when you transform?"

"You have no idea. It takes almost an hour, and it's excruciatingly painful. Then the return to human form is almost as bad. I have to reabsorb all my flight feathers and reshape my arms into human arms again."

"Hang on a minute. I have to have a conversation with my agent. Let me see what we can do about all this." Dani sat back down and closed his eyes.

"White Fang, have you been following along with our present conversation?"

"I'm here, stud-muffin. You're at it again, I see. You couldn't keep a military secret if it were given to you as a 'burn-before-reading' message."

"Yeah, yeah. I'm building a team, and at least I've gotten us out of here. What I need from you is another assessment for a new recruit. Selena has bird DNA she can trigger to morph herself into a bird, and fly. We're going to use that ability, but first we have to make it better. Right now, it's too painful for her. You've got pain management in the MIL-SPEC, so we'll have to implement that. We also will need the tanglenet computer system set up. Are you following?"

"I get you. The first step in any of this will be setting up the quad-core metabionic tanglenet system, but even before that, you will have to give me an order to release the MIL-SPEC_AP to the Selena Unit."

"Got it. Release the MIL-SPEC_AP to the Selena Unit."

"Understood. The procedure will be implemented. Further instructions, Sir?"

"Yes, besides making the morphing procedure less painful, we may need to increase her strength somehow. She has the shape of a sixteen-year-old girl, when she's not a bird that is, so she's bigger than I am. We should be able to make her stronger."

"This will be a complicated build. Can you give me permission to use the other quad-core metabionic tanglenet system available to us for calculation and rendering purposes?"

"You mean the one you built in Roni? Sure, you're authorized to use that. Oh hey, let me check something with Selena. Hang on."

Dani opened his eyes. "We're working out the details, and I just thought of something. Selena, how old do you want to be?"

"What do you mean how old do I want to be? I'm sixteen. I can't change that."

"I mean, how old do you want to be for the rest of your life? You're sixteen now, but do you want to be sixteen forever?"

"Oh. Well, I know I don't want to be ten. That would be too small. I'm not sure whether I want to be older than sixteen. What do you think, should I wait until I'm twenty-one or something?"

"My sister Lori is twenty-one, and has been for a few years. I don't think it will make any difference. Being sixteen, you could pass for twenty-one and vice-versa. Easiest to do right now would be to freeze you at sixteen. To go for twenty-one might mean a few more years of painful transformations, while you age normally."

"Oh, no more pain please. I like being sixteen, even if it means that I'm a little too old for you. I think I could live with being sixteen for a long time."

"Not too old for me, I assure you. Lori is twenty-one, and we get along fine. At our last party, she told people I was her doctor. It worked out nicely."

"Sixteen it is then. Wow! I get to be sixteen for the rest of my life, and no more pain when I transform! This is wonderful!"

"Well there's more too, but let me get back to work."

"More?" Selena said, but Dani had already closed his eyes.

"White Fang, here are your instructions for the build. The Selena Unit will have her nanobots modified to implement the MIL-SPEC_AP. She will remain sixteen in appearance and functions. The MIL-SPEC_AP will have to accommodate being able to change from human to her bird-form, and will supplement her strength in bird-form. Then it will also need to accommodate changing back to her human form. Unfortunately, that will mean that her skin can not be strengthened the way you described mine would be, since she has to grow feathers from it."

"Acknowledged, Sir. I will begin the process with the quad-core metabionic tanglenet system, implement the communications protocols, prepare the pain management procedures, and modify or create nanobots to lock down the Selena Genome structure for morphing and being a constant sixteen years old."

"That sounds right. Are you aware of anything I've missed?"

"You have not assigned an agent name to the Selena Unit."

"Oh, right, hmm. How about 'Top Gun'?"

"Very good, Sir. You can fill me in on armament capabilities later. White Fang out."

Dani opened his eyes. Armament capabilities?

Selena was watching him. "You said there's more. What more?"

Dani looked between them. "Each of us will have an advanced computer system built inside us. I don't even know where it is, but I assume it's up near the brain. It facilitates communications between your Application program and yourself, but it also makes possible communications between your computers and mine. Essentially, we'll all be mutual mind-readers."

"Really? I had no idea." Roni said.

"Your system is still growing." He looked at Selena, "Your system is having its seeds designed. It will be a week or two before we can play around with the possibilities, but I'm told they are tremendous."

"Like what?" Selena asked.

"You'll always know where I am, and Roni too. You'll be able to talk with us silently and no one will know it's happening. I'm told we can even send images back and forth. Again, there's more, but I'm not sure I can believe what I've been told about that."

"So what's so unbelievable?" asked Roni.

"My agent told me that once we've mastered all the parameters of how our system works, we will be able to control each other's hands and legs, and even see out of each other's eyes. As I said, it doesn't sound possible."

"So we'll be married then." Prompted Selena.

"Maybe more than married, I'd say." Dani responded.

"How far apart … How much range are we talking about?" inquired Roni.

"We don't know yet. We'll have to experiment. So far I haven't been able to get very far away from you, but I haven't reached a limit yet."

"Ana's going to be disappointed." Roni said.

"That's going to be another question." Dani replied.

"I don't need to be a mind-reader to know what *that* question is."

"Who is Anna?" said Selena.

"Anastasia; legally my foster cousin. In reality, she's the mother of my adoptive mother. It gets complicated." Roni noted.

"Ana shows the apparent age of thirteen. I met her at Malcolm's. He's fourteen, by the way, actual age." Dani watched her. "You'll like him."

"So why will Ana be disappointed?"

"We had gotten pretty close. I was living with her for a while just before Roni got adopted. I suspect that she will want to join our little close-knit group."

"Ah!" Selena said in recognition. She looked at Dani. "You were living with her?"

"She's a woman of means. She's a sponsor for Malcolm, one of his financiers. She and I discovered that we had something in common, neither of us being what we seem. I like her. She pretends to be the child of her own daughter."

"So it's complicated then."

"Yeah." Roni admitted.

"So you're thinking that she and I will get along like cats and ... birds?"

Dani shrugged. "I don't think there will be a problem. Ana is very mature and calm of spirit. She liked teasing her daughter by flaunting her relationship with me, but she doesn't seem to get too excited by things."

"So if I were to cling to your arm all evening?"

"She would give you a kiss on the cheek and say have fun."

"I think I like her already."

"That was my reaction as well. She's a very nice person. In the role she plays, she hides in the background while Alicia makes all the corporate deals."

"Hmm. I'm going to need some guidance. I've been leading a sheltered life."

"And now here you are, just ready to step out of the nest and you're married already." Dani said.

"Married?"

"Our little close-knit group."

"So I might need a big little sister." Selena nodded.

"She's that for all of us, I think." Dani admitted.

"Well, I want to meet her, but if you think you should invite her to join the group, I won't complain."

"It could be useful. We're going to explore space together. Another form of communication could be important."

"Going into space … I don't think that would be right for me."

"Scared of heights?" Roni suggested.

She smiled. "What good would wings be in space?"

"Communication back to the ground could be important too. It would give us a chance to test our range." Dani pointed out.

"I'm pretty sure that would be out of range. To communicate at that distance you'd be burning out your brain with the transmitter power."

"Speed of light delays too. But don't be concerned if you have to stay behind. We'll get Mister Rob to give you some assignments. You can be like Miss Alicia and earn money for your 'children' while they're having fun."

Selena laughed. "I'm ready to see you dance now," she said with a predatory smile.

"Mister Roni, if you please, we'll need some music." Dani went up the stairs to get into his costume.

27

A phone started to ring

Dani took his clothes off again and examined the leather thong underwear.

He had actually been teasing, but Selena being Selena, now he had to live with it. He smiled.

Dani arranged the contraption on his meager hips. Yes it covered his pubic area, just barely. But the leather running up between his butt cheeks was a little distracting.

Dancing naked was easy and he was used to it. This could actually be an irritant. Oh well, a short dance should be fun anyway.

After securing the straps and doing a bit of stretching, Dani decided he was ready. The feel of the minimal cover was intriguing. The garment could not be more securely attached to him if it had been applied with adhesive. It was like wearing an eye-patch on the other end of the sight path. Funny how a tiny scrap of clothing made one look even more naked.

The music had started. Roni had made a good selection. It was show time!

Dani sprang out from behind the bookcase, toes extended and hands raised. He landed and stood still for a beat. Then he strutted proudly forward as if leading a parade.

He realized something. He had danced in costume before, sometimes using a full body stocking. This felt similar. Although almost all of his body was showing, it felt as though nothing of consequence could be seen. On the male body, there were arms and legs, a head, and if the genital area was covered, really nothing else to be concerned about.

He danced, springing in time with the crescendos and twirling, lungeing, actually enjoying his movement. He had danced to this music before, but it was designed for more of a group. It didn't matter. Usually the eyes of the audience would be on the principle dancer.

Dani had good form, and he hadn't forgotten much of his training. He was enjoying his performance, and he was confident that his audience appreciated it as well.

The music came to a close, and he folded gracefully into the floor, relaxing in what to many would be an awkward position, but was very elegant to see.

Roni and Selena were clapping wildly. Both had enjoyed the show, but Selena had tears in her eyes.

"Oh, Dani! So marvelous! You are just exquisite. Such a miracle of delight!" She pulled him to her and rubbed his bare flesh with carefree abandon. She bent his head backwards and kissed him on the lips, rubbing his posterior and pulling it upwards. Dani let his weight fall into her arms, dropping his arms down as if he had fainted.

She brought her hand to his chest, rubbing across his stomach and lower abdomen.

"You even smell delightful!" she stood him upright again and hugged him, rubbing his back energetically.

Roni stepped up, pulling Dani into another hug. He buried his head in Dani's neck again, sniffling. "Oh, Dani! Everything you do makes me weep with joy, just to be near you!"

Dani accepted their accolades, and stood calmly for a moment.

"So, how did you like my outfit?" he said, standing straight and putting his arms out to the side.

Selena reached out and stroked across the smooth surface. "I notice it fits you quite well."

"Thank you." Dani stretched again, as if straightening out wrinkles in his garment. "Yes, it's a nice fit. Now, where were we? Oh, yes, our coming space adventure." He began pacing back and forth like a lecturer up on the stage of an assembly hall.

"Malcolm wants to pin down the final design parameters so the ship can begin taking shape in the production facility. We aren't quite there yet. I think we should suggest to him that we only authorize the precise dimensions of the outer hull. It will take some time before that would prevent us from making necessary modifications to the interior."

Selena stood back a pace. "Should I be taking notes?"

"No, no, I'm just thinking to myself. Say, when you're prepared to leave here, have you decided what you want to take?"

"I'm going to take my new clothes, except for the panties." Roni suggested.

Dani nodded to him. He continued striding back and forth, as if busy making complex executive decisions.

Selena stopped him with another full-on-lips kiss. "Never mind that. If you have nothing better to do, you have some phone calls to make, and then you can start dinner. I'll go pack."

Dani stood upright, raising his arm, "A phone, a phone. My kingdom for a phone!" In a kitchen cupboard, a phone started to ring.

Dani looked that way. "Son of a gun!" He walked into the kitchen.

o-o-o

The smell of food drew the inhabitants into the kitchen. There they found Dani still walking around wearing nothing but a patch and a string.

Selena reached out to stroke his smooth flank as he stood near her. Dani paused, accepting the caress, and then moved on.

"So how long are you going to wear that thing, and what point are you trying to make?" She asked the young boy.

He grinned at her. "Honestly, it's easy to forget that it's there, except that for some reason I feel even more comfortable with it on than with it off." He looked down. "Strange, huh? What I've noticed is that I'm less conscious of being practically naked, even though I'm quite used to being so."

158

He looked up. "Hey, it doesn't bother you, does it? I can always take it off."

"That wouldn't necessarily make things better, you know. We are after all about to eat dinner. You may dress as you please, and I will ogle as I choose." She patted his buns once more.

"Oh good." Dani continued bustling about the kitchen.

Selena shook her head. Roni nodded.

"I don't think you'll get him to change anything once he's tried it." He noted. "Still, we love him, and that won't change."

"And he's going to be the leader of our group, and he'll be able to read our minds. I predict wonderful things will be happening."

"That's fairly normal when Dani is involved. I'll predict he'll have both you and Ana in his bed the first evening you meet."

Selena sat up straight. "I am looking forward to meeting new people."

Roni grinned. "Funny how what I thought was a case of being kidnapped has turned into a rescue mission."

"My knight in shining armor," Selena pointed.

"Kinda dull armor, actually," Dani replied, "but at least it's comfortable. I really didn't expect that."

"Stick with me, kid," Selena responded, "You'll learn a lot."

Dani stopped to lean over and kiss her. "Damsels in this dress, I will always stop for."

Selena rolled her eyes. "I'm not wearing anything like that, ever."

Dani smiled. "We might still come up with something special for you." He looked over at Roni. "Have you heard from Captain Obvious yet?"

Roni shook his head. They ate in silence for a while.

After the dinner was mostly complete, Dani went over their plans. "We're scheduled to arrive at Malcolm's this evening. He'll put us up. Tomorrow sometime Ana will join us. What's our decision on bringing her into the group?" Dani studied their faces.

"How could we not?" Roni said.

"Why should we not?" Selena pointed out.

"I don't think I've mentioned that we will all be in mortal danger at some point because of this adventurism."

"Weren't we precisely there this very morning?" Roni submitted.

"We'll be inviting Ana in as well."

"It still should be her choice." Roni said reasonably. "She has already accepted the dangers of space travel in an unproven craft."

"I don't know her, but I doubt that she would want the decision made for her." Selena smiled. "When was the decision made for me?"

"You can blame me for that," Dani admitted, "I volunteered you."

Selena shook her head. "No, it was already decided long before that, and I wasn't even asked."

"You mean, how you were selected for this project?"

"I was ten. Like you." She pushed her food away. "Not as experienced. I fell prey to a recruiter. She was an older woman, supposedly offering food aid to victims of natural disasters. I showed up there with no relatives and no records. Funny thing is, I qualified precisely because I was undernourished and underweight. I was exactly what she was looking for."

Selena looked away. "All she had to do was feed me, and fill my head with lies about a wonderful opportunity. I would be working with brilliant people trying to help humanity solve global problems. I would be their subject for scientific research."

"The first tests were easy. They wanted to find out how well I adapted to genetic manipulation. They were all so happy! I was perfect for their program, although it might involve just a little bit of discomfort for me."

She smiled through tears. "I worked with them. I accepted the pain and smiled to show I was okay, but I really wasn't. I didn't want to be thrown out of the program. After all, I was perfect for them. Perfect. What I didn't realize was that perfect simply meant no one would miss me and no one would come looking for me."

Selena looked up. "If I died in the research, they would simply start over. I was perfect."

"It didn't cost as much at first. They kept me hidden at little expense. This all came much later, after the whole genetic sequence had been modified bit by bit. It must have been a different branch of research. Mister Jennison said he inherited this. I think he inherited me and my program also. You did him a favor. I don't think he knew what to do with me."

Dani held her hands. "This doesn't seem anything like what Genano was doing. This is more expensive, but more primitive in the technology. Genano would have been more test tube and fewer tests."

She looked at him with tears in her eyes. "But it worked! That was the miracle! I just wasn't strong enough. I couldn't even fly until three years ago. The first years I went through all the pain of transforming and all I could do was flap my wings. But then, even after I was able to fly, I wasn't strong enough. I could barely stay in the air, mostly by gliding and using thermals. I can fly here in a controlled environment, but out in the world I would be crashing just from turbulence. I've gotten stronger, but not strong enough. I represent a colossal failure."

"You're a wonderful failure. That's how we got together. Rob put all his failures in one basket." Dani smiled at her. "I wasn't supposed to get my military upgrade. That was an accident, and Mr. Jennison was getting the blame for it."

Dani closed his eyes. "White Fang, how goes the Selena Project?"

"In truth, slowly. This project is much more complex. We don't have comparison DNA profiles to check against, and matching it to yours doesn't work. You don't have bird DNA in your genome to compare. But we know or assume that her transformation works, because she can fly. One procedure that should work properly is the non-aging prospect. We know precisely where to make the changes for that. The proper way to do this, once the Selena Unit has a functioning quad-core metabionic tanglenet system will be to study the transformation basis to see where nanobot strength boosting will benefit most."

"So we'll have to ask her to transform after the tanglenet goes live?"

"Yes Sir."

"And before her pain management can be made effective."

"Yes Sir."

"How will we get the metabionic tanglenet computer system started in her?"

"You may have to kiss her rather assertively, if you can bring yourself to do that. Sir."

"Understood. Carry on."

Dani opened his eyes. "We're going to fix you up, but it's still going to hurt a few more times. Good news and bad news, I guess."

Selena smiled. "At least I'll be among friends."

28

More than a mere handshake

Roni was astonished at the change in Malcolm's size. His hesitation gave him the delay needed to remember that while Malcolm was still a growing boy, he himself had become a shrunken man, who now presented himself as a boy under the name of Roni Winthrope.

"Welcome back, Dani!" Malcolm greeted them. He was dressed in evening attire, which in this mountain retreat, involved pajamas, slippers, and a robe. Dani remembered that the party temperature had been much warmer.

"Thank you, Malcolm, especially considering the late notice, and even later arrival. May I present Roni Winthrope, the adopted son of our mutual friend Alicia Winthrope, and the equivalent of my adopted cousin, and another friend we've recently met, Miss Selena Sanchez, who has been our hostess for a recent spa vacation.

"Greetings, Roni, welcome aboard. I am very pleased to meet you, Miss Sanchez. Dani, I have rooms available for all of you at 9, 10, and 11B upstairs. Use them as you wish, and for as long as you wish."

"Thank you, Malcolm. My adopted mother had many wonderful things to say about you, but she especially emphasized what a wonderful host you were." Roni shook Malcolm's hand.

"Thank you for your hospitality, Mr. Horowitz, I can only hope to repay it someday." Selena offered her hand as well, but Malcolm drew her into a friendly hug.

"I know that any friend of Dani's would expect more than a mere handshake, Miss Sanchez."

"Please, call me Selena. I've almost forgotten I had a last name."

"Then you must call me Malcolm, as all my friends do." Malcolm smiled at her as he stepped back. "Now, knowing that it's late, at least in this time zone, I will give you the opportunity to immediately retire, or you may refresh yourselves any way you wish. The kitchen is open twenty-four hours a day, as are all the facilities. I, however, only operate about seventeen hours a day, and this is approaching my seventeenth hour."

"Thank you, Malcolm. We appreciate your staying up to greet us, and we're very grateful for your hospitality." Dani shook his hand again.

Malcolm waved and took his leave.

"Anyone want a midnight snack?" Dani asked. "The bedrooms here are like a hotel suite. You can even request automated deliveries. Malcolm's place here is like a manufacturing center. He has the capability and the equipment to make many of the devices used in his research, all it requires is the sending of the appropriate file information. That includes being able to make clothes in any style and fabric you choose. He even has an industrial knitting loom that can make whole dresses and anything else seamlessly and in any size. You could arrive here the way I usually dress and outfit yourself with a whole wardrobe. But the room service can also bring you food items from the kitchen."

"I want to see the fabled former quarters of Doctor Thornton, but I suppose I should wait a bit to be more respectful about it." Roni said. "Other than that, and a minor snack craving, I'm ready to go to bed."

"I stayed in 11B before. I'll take that one." Dani said. "Selena, what is your pleasure?"

"Oh, that's an open ended question. Let's take a walk and look at the bedrooms." Selena smiled at him.

Dani led them through the corridors and up the winding stairs. Everything was hewn out of the solid rock of the mountain, and it gave the impression of being an ages-old castle.

"Here's nine, for whoever wants it," Dani said.

"I'll take it." Roni said. "I may try to get Malcolm to let me use the library quarters, but that can wait. A nice bed is more important at the moment. Good night, you two."

Selena took his arm. "Show me your room, Dani. I'm tired, too, but I like having familiar things around me when I'm in an unfamiliar place."

Dani grinned. "Okay, that's one way to put it." He led Selena to 11B.

The room was exactly as he remembered it. Dani put his small bundle of new clothes on the dresser and tossed the clothes he was wearing into the laundry chute. Malcolm's automatic equipment included automatic laundry management. He walked over to stand at the view window and study the minor changes in the fields of the village below.

"It's very picturesque." Selena was standing beside him. "Aren't you worried that someone out there might have a telescope?"

Dani grinned. "As if I care. But to answer your question, this is a simulated window; it's just conveying the image from a camera on the outside of the mountain. No one can see us. The curtains are just to keep out the morning light."

"Malcolm seems to like his technology." Selena said.

"That's what makes him Malcolm. He likes manufacturing; I like computers and nano-technology." He looked over at her, "You should probably take advantage here to study aerodynamics and flight characteristics."

Selena moved back to the laundry panel, and began removing her clothes as well. "I doubt if I could do more than make an interesting crash site in these mountains."

Dani watched her. "Malcolm has a helicopter landing pad, if you change your mind. But I think you should wait until we can maybe augment your strength before you try."

Selena turned to face him, looking down at her chest. "I don't have breasts when I transform, just in case you were wondering if the cold air would make my nipples stand out."

Dani walked toward her, "Your nipples are outstanding anyway,

Selena. I like them a lot." He approached her and gave her a hug, burying his face in her surprisingly firm but shapely bosom.

Selena rubbed his back, appreciating the warmth and softness of his skin. "Let's go to bed. I just want to cuddle with you and hold you close."

Dani led her to the bed, climbing in first so that she could be closer to the bathroom if she needed it.

Selena pulled the covers down and lay down beside him, pulling him close to her. She kissed his neck and wrapped her arm around his chest. "Good night, Dani," she said softly.

o-o-o-o-o

Dani and Selena walked together down to the dining room for breakfast. Malcolm was there, having some coffee.

"I've been hoping to see you soon, Dani. I've been waiting for your approval on the ship design."

"I took a little time this morning helping Selena choose a new dress. Your knittery makes a tempting shopping choice."

Malcolm rose to bow appreciatively to the sight that Selena made. Her dress flowed around her smoothly with bands of alternating colors and a scattering of embroidered flowers merged into the weave. Its clinging nature made it apparent but not obvious that she was not wearing a brassiere. "Good morning, dear lady, you make my investment a worthy one indeed."

Selena gave a brief curtsy. "Thank you, my lord. Your hospitality exceeds my ability to express my thanks."

Malcolm gave a wave of dismissal and a gesture to their seats. He sat again and looked once more at Dani. "So you were saying about the ship? If you're quite finished with your spa vacation, that is."

"Slave driver," Dani said humorously, "Spa vacation is a good story in itself, but I have been working on my assignment, I assure you. I don't see anything that will keep us on the ground. There are some minor discrepancies in the way it all goes together, but I should be able to give you a complete report at the end of the week."

Dani picked up a tablet and glanced over it, choosing several items from the breakfast menu and some tea. He showed Selena his selection for her approval and doubled the order at her nod.

Malcolm had relaxed back in his seat once more. "Well, that's a little delay, but good news overall. I have to tell you I've been biting my nails over how much time this is taking. I want to do it right but I thought it would go faster than this."

"Maybe you need some smaller projects to work on in the meantime. I've been thinking about a couple of industrial projects that I could really use your help with, if you're interested."

"Oh," Malcolm perked up. "What did you have in mind?"

"I'd like to make a fusion-powered helicopter, using your power design, and I think I might need a combination glider and sweep-wing supersonic craft as well."

"A fusion-powered helicopter? Ah, you're going for unlimited range, of course. Yes, that sounds like a good idea!"

"It probably sounds like a military application, but I'd want good lifting capacity and storage, along with almost silent landing and takeoff."

"How many rotors?"

"In my mind, I'm seeing three. I realize that might be a little complex internally, but it should be very useful if it works the way I think it will." Dani mused.

"Hmm. Our power plant should be able to handle that. Do you think you could submit some drawings of what you have in mind? We could send it to the engineers to go over and get back to us."

"Sure thing. The other craft might need more of their input anyway. I want to be able to go fast for a long distance, and then loiter inconspicuously for a long time."

"What are you getting into, Dani? That definitely sounds like a military mission."

Dani shrugged, "Or taking a bunch of ecologists to a remote jungle with no landing strip."

Malcolm scratched his chin, "Are you thinking of using fusion power plants instead of fuel burners?"

"I think it's possible. Fan-jets are mostly fans. Their motors just need power. Too bad we don't have a big wind tunnel to test it."

Malcolm waved his hand again. "I can get access to one. Especially if you might consider licensing the concept to some agencies."

"It would be tough to keep it secret, so why not?"

"Hmm. Why haven't I had you on the payroll for a year or two?"

Their breakfasts arrived. Dani and Selena attended to that for a moment.

Dani looked up. "Did you want to share credit for the ideas, or would you have to own it for yourself?"

"I've been trying to figure out what my obligation is to you for the power upgrade anyway. I don't have any problem sharing. What would you need?"

"What would you say to an even split, and you can put me on your payroll backdated to the beginning of the year?"

"Even split from the gross or the net?"

"We're friends, Malcolm. You know the answer to that."

"Hmm. What salary then?"

"Something in balance. If you don't expect much profit, a small salary, and if you make oodles, you can spread the wealth. As I said, we're friends."

"You trust me then?"

"Implicitly and without reservation." Dani went back to his breakfast for the moment.

Malcolm smiled and called for more coffee.

"You fellows are having a nice chat." Selena said quietly.

"Sorry to ignore you, Miss." Malcolm said. "Dani said you were his hostess for a spa vacation?"

She smiled. "He was being generous. He and Roni went swimming and out on hikes. They were able to eat a nutritious and varied diet and enjoy quiet downtime with reading and listening to music. It was very peaceful."

"I could use something like that, but I can never get away." He lamented.

"From what I can tell, you could do that right here." Selena said calmly.

"Before you try to hire her away from me, be advised that she's on my team already, as is Roni." Dani interjected.

"And you're on mine." Malcolm smiled.

"Well, maybe. But you would have to help me pay their salaries."

"How would you like to be a hostess here?" Malcolm asked Selena.

"That's what I suggested to Lori." Dani said.

"I could hire her!" Selena said brightly.

"You haven't met her." Dani pointed out.

"I have," said Malcolm. "This sounds promising."

"This sounds complicated." Dani groused.

"Most of my staff seem to live in fear of me," Malcolm said, nodding toward the kitchen. "It might be fun to have friends around who know how to be productive too."

"Speaking of which, my friend Roni is interested in Doctor Thornton's quarters as a place to set up his research, if that's still available."

"What's his field?" Malcolm asked, "We've missed old Thorny."

"Not too far from Doctor Thornton's specialty actually, but with a newer attitude and optimism." Dani said. "I depend on him for analysis in depth and common-sense advice."

"And he's on your team too?"

"Already on the team." Dani nodded.

"So I wouldn't have to pay him any more salary than I pay you?"

"Considering that I don't know what you're offering me, I think it's safe to say he will accept that."

"Okay, if he'll respect what we've been doing with Thorny's quarters, which is to treat it as a research facility, then he can move in there if he wants to."

"Wow! You guys move fast!" Selena said in wonder. "Roni's probably still asleep!"

"I'm sure you'll find him to be invaluable. I consider him to be almost a brother, though technically he's more of a cousin."

29

It never came up

"There he is!"

Dani turned to face the door.

Alicia and Anastasia were coming through it with big smiles on their faces. Quickly, Dani messaged White Fang to get Roni moving.

"And here's Ana," Dani said softly to Selena. He rose to greet the women.

Although Alicia held back for proper decorum, Ana ran to him and embraced him. "You had us so worried! Where have you been?"

Dani picked up the larger girl and swung her around. "I'm happy to see you too, sweetheart, but Roni and I had to stop and rescue a damsel in distress from a baleful dungeon."

Malcolm had come around the table and was standing by Selena. Stage-whispering, he said, "I heard they were having a spa vacation."

Selena responded the same way, "First time I've heard my place called a dungeon."

Dani winked at them. "Ana, I have someone for you to meet." He put her down and directed her to Selena. "This is my friend and new business partner, Miss Selena Sanchez. Selena, this is my good friend Anastasia Winthrope."

"Thank you for taking care of my friend, Miss Sanchez."

"Please call me Selena. I had to take good care of my rescuer. At one point he really needed a bath."

Ana grinned, "I can believe that. But thank you again, he seems to be fine now."

"You ladies should have some breakfast. As usual, Malcolm's buying."

Malcolm gestured toward the table.

Before Alicia had gotten even halfway to the breakfast table, Roni came sliding in through the doorway in his stocking feet.

Alicia turned and held her arms out. Roni went to her to be hugged.

"Just in time for breakfast, as usual," Dani teased.

"Welcome, everyone. Come and eat. I, unfortunately, have to go to work." He waved and made his exit amidst the clamor.

Dani guided Ana around the table to sit opposite Selena's location, while Selena resumed her seat. Alicia came to sit beside Ana, and Roni sat down beside Selena.

"Nice entrance," Selena said.

"You should have seen me jumping out of bed!"

"At least you had a bed to sleep in. You weren't allowed to in my dungeon."

"What?" Roni stared.

"You snooze, you lose, Roni." Dani said, "Try to keep up."

Selena looked over to Alicia. "The boys came to visit me a few days ago. They convinced me to come here with them, and here we are. There are more ways to tell the story, but that's the gist. I'm Selena."

"I am pleased to meet you, Selena. Thank you for returning my wayward son."

"It was my pleasure, Ma'am. He's a delightful boy."

Roni was blushing a deep red. "I think I'll just eat." He reached out for a tablet.

Ana and Alicia stared at him for a moment, and then looked around to see if anyone else had noticed his gaffe.

Seeing their reaction, Roni tried to cover. "I guess this is how we place our orders, right?"

Ana said, "That's right, cousin. You're a fast learner."

Dani had resumed his seat beside Selena. "What do you think about Malcolm? Is he too young for you?"

"He seems quite the businessman. So are you, for that matter. Did I get it right that I'm working for you?"

"You're working *with* me. You may also be working for Malcolm, at least part of the time."

"Yeah. It's complicated."

Dani shrugged his shoulders.

"Malcolm said you would be able to use Doctor Thornton's old quarters if you want to. He said you had to respect it as a research facility." Selena said to Roni.

Roni looked at her, and then over to Dani, who nodded at him. "Thanks," Roni said.

"So you got the message then," Dani said softly and silently inside Roni's head.

"Yeah, thanks for that." Roni replied the same way. "Scared the liver out of me."

"I figured you were ready by now. Malcolm wants us to get to work."

Roni nodded, and turned once more to the menu pad.

"Your sister is on her way too." Ana told Dani. "She wants to be able to reassure your parents that you are indeed okay."

"I was in good hands," Dani said. "There was no need to worry."

Ana turned to Selena. "Okay, now that it's just us girls, you can tell us the whole story."

Dani said, "Hey, what about me and Roni?"

"Oh shush, I want to hear the truth."

Selena laughed at Dani's downtrodden expression. "My place," she said, "is a little difficult to get to. Nevertheless, these two vagrants showed up one day, like Hansel and Gretel ready to start eating my gingerbread house. I pointed out to them that the whole forest was nothing but fruit trees and they went off to eat something else. Then I found them shaking and shivering after they got caught out in the rain."

She smiled at Dani. "So I had to take them in and get them cleaned up. Now I noticed that they had nothing more than the clothes on their backs, so I had to face the embarrassment of two naked savages rampaging around in my little cottage until I could get them calmed down and asleep."

"You know, I remember it slightly different than that." Dani protested.

"I believe you were told to be quiet, young man." Alicia said sternly.

"Yes, Ma'am."

"Of course, while they were asleep they were just perfect little angels, but then they woke up, and this one got into my perfume and the other one made a mess of the library. Why, I even saw them putting my underwear on and wearing it!"

"Hey, I like the way she tells this story!" said Roni.

"Traitor," Dani said.

"And your house?" inquired Ana.

"Truthfully, it will never be the same," Selena answered.

"Well boys, what do you have to say for yourselves?" scolded Alicia.

"Sorry, Miss Selena," said Dani.

"Sorry." Whispered Roni in turn.

Selena leaned over and kissed Dani full on the mouth, holding the kiss for a long, indecorous moment, and then turned to kiss Roni in precisely the same way.

"I love these boys." Selena said happily.

"Welcome to the family," responded Ana with a smile.

They continued bantering through a long breakfast and then Ana came around to fetch Dani, while Alicia took Roni aside. "Come Selena, let's have a stroll around," Ana said to the girl. "I'll bet they haven't given you a proper tour yet."

Selena wiped her mouth and got up to follow them.

"One of my favorite spots is the indoor pool. It's where people are willing to share their darkest secrets." Ana led the others into the darkened pool area. Dani wondered for a moment how the plants in there stayed alive through the constant semi-darkness.

Ana took her clothes off and folded them to place them on a bench. She looked at Dani, who without a word followed suit. They looked at each other.

Selena slipped her dress over her head and folded it also, placing it on another bench. Then she removed some knit panties that Dani had helped her make just this morning, along with eleven other pairs.

Dani and Ana sat together at the poolside. Dani patted a spot next to him and Selena joined them.

"Selena's body is amazing, Ana. You should feel her breasts. It's no wonder she's willing to go without a bra. Her breasts are firm and wonderful without one."

"Thank you, Dani. I'm not sure Ana wanted to hear that."

"To the contrary," replied Ana, "I'm pleased that Dani is willing to share how he feels about you. If he wanted to keep his feelings secret, then I would think he did not trust me."

"When you say feelings, you mean how I think about someone, and not what I do with my hands, right?" Dani reached over to put his hand on Selena's breast and caress it.

Ana watched them both with a smile. "He's a tease, isn't he?" She looked out over the water and splashed her feet to watch the ripples spread. "This is where we first got naked together, and decided that we would have sex later. I guess you could say he convinced me."

"Wait, there's something I don't understand. Are you saying you've had sex with Dani? How would that work?"

Ana looked back at Dani, "You've dragged this girl halfway around the world, and you haven't had sex with her?"

"It never came up." Dani said lamely.

"I could smack you," Ana said. She looked over at Selena. "He's been pretending to be a ten-year-old again, hasn't he?"

"But ..." Selena stared, "isn't he?"

"He's what he wants to be. He can turn it on and off." She looked at Dani. "Stand up, Dani. Do it."

Dani shrugged, and stood up. He turned to face away from the pool, and he started getting an erection.

Even without a touch or a caress, he willed a change on himself, and it happened that easily. Soon his little inch-long nubbin was a respectable gentleman.

Ana looked at Selena, "After you." She gestured an invitation.

Selena reached out and touched it gently; pushing it and having it swing rigidly back into position.

"I've never touched one before," Selena said.

"Put your hand around it and squeeze it gently," Ana suggested.

Selena wrapped her hand around it and squeezed her fingers gently. Dani put his hands up on the back of his head and spread his feet apart.

Ana reached out and cupped her hand around his scrotum, holding it up against his body in the same way the fleshy sack always held its contents.

"Move your hand around," Ana told Selena. "Dani, show her what the fluid looks like."

In a moment, a glistening droplet of clear fluid emerged at the tip.

"Spread that around," Ana commanded again.

Selena obediently performed her task, rubbing and stimulating the boy with her fingers and his fluid.

"Now, if you decide to have sex with Dani, he can provide all the sensations of having sex that you want. He's been holding out on you if you thought he couldn't."

"I never said one way or the other, but Selena is still a virgin." Dani said in his own defense.

"What does that mean?" Selena asked.

"He has a point," Ana responded, glancing upward, "and it isn't that one. When a girl has sex for the first time, she breaks or ruptures a membrane inside her called the hymen. It could be painful, but it's often also a significant social event, even though it doesn't normally occur in public."

Selena was continuing to stroke her hand over the slippery shaft. Dani stood still and calm.

"In some cultures, it's required that a bride be a virgin," Ana said. "Dani's right that this should be your choice and that it should be explained to you."

"Well, suppose it doesn't matter to me," Selena asked, her voice dropping down a little into a slight huskiness.

"Well, in that case," Ana said, rising to stand in front of Dani.

"You need to think about it." She placed a hand on Dani's chest and pushed him into the pool.

Dani turned his fall into a graceful back flip, arcing into the water with at least one mast still erect. He swam leisurely to the other end, turned, and swam back.

"Wash your hand off," Ana instructed.

Selena rinsed her hand in the pool. Ana reached around her and put her hand on Selena's breast, squeezing it gently and fondling the nipple.

"Dani is right. You do have very firm breasts. If I were you, I would never wear a bra."

Dani was watching them. He climbed out by the diving board and dove back in again, stroking smoothly across and then returning once more.

Selena stood up. Ana approached her and kissed her on the lips.

"You have a wonderful, very attractive body. You should think about whether you want to discard your virginity or maybe be so foolish as to save it for someone like Malcolm. He's going to need a wife in a few years; I could see it being you."

"Not you?"

"No, I don't think so. I'm going to be thirteen forever. Malcolm's interest in me has already come and gone. He will be looking for someone more mature, more wifely. Someone like you."

"I'm going to be … if things work out the way we think it will … I'm going to be sixteen forever. Won't that be too young too?"

Dani continued swimming and diving.

"No, dear. That would be almost perfect. You should see Malcolm when Dani's sister comes around. He just melts. She's twenty-one, twenty-one forever, that is. It's not a bad choice. You might even think about it yourself."

"No. We've talked about that and it's … well, just not in the cards. It's sixteen for me. I'll have to settle for that."

"Settle for that, she says. Honey, there are eighty-year-old women out there who would give anything they could possess to be sixteen again, just for a little while. A famous writer once said that no woman ever grows older than sixteen in her heart. You'll get to live that wondrous dream."

"So you're pushing me toward Malcolm?"

"No, I don't want to push you anywhere. I won't even push you away from Dani or Roni. You can set your own sights. I'm just pointing out the choices for you, hoping you'll be able to see them too."

"You sound like somebody's mother," Selena said with a smile.

"I *am* somebody's mother! Alicia is my daughter!"

"Oh, right, I forgot. It's complicated."

Ana smiled, and hugged her, and kissed her again.

"Come on Dani, before you get waterlogged."

"I was logged before I went in the water," came Dani's plaintive voice.

Ana smiled. She looked at Selena, who was also smiling.

"He's such a brat," Ana said, "you can have him tonight if you want him."

Selena looked up. "I love him. I don't think that will change. But just for now I think I'll wait a bit. It's not like I don't have other things to worry about anyway."

"Anything you want to talk about, Dearie, you just come to me."

"I will, thanks." Selena kissed her in return.

Dani had found a towel to dry with and had gotten dressed once more. The girls followed suit.

Ana led them out into the corridor again. "You know, I still have to unpack. I'll see you both in a bit. Cheerio!" She left for the stairs.

"Feeling better?" Dani asked.

"Feeling a little smarter, maybe. She's quite a person, isn't she?"

"That she is. I love her too."

"You make that sound like you're saying I love her."

"We both love her. Don't try to argue with me about it. We both, Ana and I, love you as well. Never argue with people who are older and wiser than you."

Selena kissed him. She rocked him back on his heels with a passionate kiss, and then she simply looked in his face. "Now what?" She asked him.

"I think I'd better go to work. Ana works miracles her way; mine take a little more effort."

"I'll go back to our room. I need to order more shoes. And I'm charging them to you!"

Dani smiled and kissed her. Then he spun away and headed off for Thorny's old rooms.

30

That's very sound advice

Roni was standing in the middle of the space, turning and staring. "Something wrong?" Dani asked.

"It's bigger than I thought. When I … uh, when Doctor Thornton moved in here, it took eight months to get everything organized. I just moved in with a single armload of clothes."

"You'll need to order more shoes. Selena just reminded me."

"Shoes," Roni mumbled, "Great."

"In the meantime, I'm going to be borrowing your brain computer. I have to finish up Malcolm's Rocket, and I also want to sketch out our new flying craft."

Roni stared at him. "What new flying craft?"

"I want a way to get us where we need to be when Rob Jennison gives us an assignment. We can hardly use surface transport or commercial air travel if we're not supposed to be there at all."

"You're going to have an Air Force?" Roni exclaimed in frustration.

"Only two. The others we'll build will be sold or leased to other agencies. Malcolm needs income to pay our salaries."

"Anyway I can help?"

Dani grinned. "Each of these vessels will be using the fusion chambers for power. Know anyone who knows something about them?"

Roni looked thoughtful, "Well, there's Wade Finnigan, Richard, Charlie …"

"And?" Dani prompted.

"And … well, me?" Roni looked startled.

"I knew there was a reason I kept you around. Other than your passable good looks and occasional peanut-buttery kisses, that is."

Roni blinked owlishly at him. "I need to get caught up on the latest developments. I've missed a few months."

"Go slow with that. You don't want them to know your secret identity."

"Oh, right. I'll just be *your* protégé then." Roni said thoughtfully.

"I'll tell them that's why I brought you in. Malcolm is going to help me pay your salary."

"When did you come across any money?"

"Just very recently, it seems I'm going to be showering in it. I have Rob Jennison and Malcolm both contributing, not to mention what we'll get for the helicopter and long-range cruiser."

"Helicopter?" Roni looked puzzled.

"Hey, do we still have a holographic imager? We'll need to show the others too. I don't want to have everyone in our tanglenet switchboard."

"Let's set up over here. Hey, how about some sandwiches?"

"I thought we just ate? Never mind, I could use some more nutrition myself. Becoming wealthy gives me an appetite." Dani looked around for a connection to the kitchen.

Ana found them after several hours. Almost empty cups and half-eaten sandwiches were covering many of the work surfaces. She cleaned up around them without their really noticing she was there.

She looked at the holoviewer. It was displaying what looked like a manta ray without a tail. Three prominent circles gave it the appearance of a masquerade adornment.

"What is this?" She asked.

Dani and Roni looked up. "Oh, hi Ana. When did you come in? Um, that's a helicopter." Dani said.

"Isn't it supposed to have a rotor?"

"It has three. That should be sufficient."

"Oh. Why are they tucked into holes like that?"

"That's to make it safer to … oh, here. Let me show you." Dani started making changes on the display.

The helicopter shrank in size, and then appearing around it in a ghost-like rendition was an airplane, with the helicopter nestled safely against its bosom.

"Ah, I see. That way you can drop the helicopter from the airplane."

"Well yeah, but primarily it's so that the helicopter can return to the airplane and dock with it."

"Dock with it? You're going to try to land a helicopter on a plane?"

"Under it, actually. Dropping it would be easier, but we'll just power up the helicopter and launch it under its own power. Then later the helicopter can fly back up and nestle into its cradle and get locked in place for a safe ride somewhere else. Simple."

"Nobody has ever done that before. Are you sure it's even possible?"

"It shouldn't be a problem, Ana. We'll practice with flight simulators and have launch and return procedures programmed into both vessels." Roni assured her.

"With this configuration, as the helicopter lines up with its cradle, its downward thrust will become a suction force pulling it up rather tightly to the bottom of the plane. Then we just lock it in place and power down the helicopter." Dani said casually.

"I see. Well, why don't you boys take a break now? You've done quite a lot for today. It's time for your dinner, and there are people who want to see your shining faces."

Dani looked at Roni. Almost as one, they said, "Yes, ma'am."

She hooked arms with them and escorted them on their way.

After washing up, the two entered the dining room again to see that not only Ana, Alicia, and Selena were waiting for them, but Malcolm and Lori as well. Lori jumped up and ran to greet Dani with a big hug.

"Don't you ever disappear like that again! You've never been out of touch like that before and nobody knew what to think or where to find you."

Dani hugged her back and kissed her several times. "And I missed you and wanted to call you too. I promise I won't disappear like that, but I can't promise I won't disappear. I will let you know beforehand next time though."

"All right. That will work, I suppose." She pulled him toward a seat.

"Have you met Selena then?" Dani asked, as the rest of the folks settled into chairs, and the kitchen staff began bringing out large bowls and platters of a generous country dinner.

"Oh yes. I can see why you were so enchanted. She's delightful!"

"Malcolm's going to give her a chance to see if she can entertain his guests the way she had us so captivated." Dani looked over at Selena to see her blush somewhat at the description. "If you remember, I had suggested you could do something like that, so now if you think you might be interested, you'll have to interview with Selena to become an assistant hostess."

"Hmm. Going to parties for a living. It sounds challenging." Lori winked at Selena, who smiled demurely.

Despite the several conversations, people managed to help themselves to a robust combination of tasty foods, almost like an impromptu Thanksgiving dinner.

"Ana tells me you've already produced some interesting schematics, Dani. I'd like to see them when you're ready to show me." Malcolm said with fork poised.

"You're welcome to see them, Malcolm, but they'll need a bit more polish, and then we'll want to get the approval of your engineers to make sure it's feasible. It's just a first draft so far."

"Intriguing idea, though. I like your imagination."

o-o-o-o-o

"So the plane is the support base for the helicopter?" Malcolm was looking at the holoviewer.

"Right. The plane can take it to the area of investigation, launch it, and then loiter until the helicopter returns."

"That's a big plane."

Dani nodded.

"Well, the helicopter, and the support base is a marketable idea.

182

But a plane that size would be hard to write off. Is there any way you could stow the helicopter and then dock another one? To carry more than one?"

Dani stood lost in thought. "Hmm. Once the helicopter is locked in place, the docking area could be raised, and a temporary floor rolled across like a pool cover. Then the first helicopter could be stowed elsewhere and the docking port returned for another."

Roni nodded. "With this size plane, because it's also a cargo plane, we could carry as many as six of the helicopters."

Malcolm grinned, "And then we could expand the market. We could sell to rescue missions, disaster relief agencies, humanitarian aid, relocation, not to mention enforcement actions."

"I'm not sure how effective it could be militarily. It's not very defensible, although it's power capability is immense." Dani admitted.

"With power, lasers could be used for defense, but that's a problem for the consumer." Malcolm continued.

"I just want to be able to visit places and not get in trouble, if I could stay invisible, that would work for me."

Malcolm studied him with a surprisingly mature-looking countenance. Dani held very still.

"Being invisible can be a way of attracting unwanted attention. For the sake of your companions, a Plan B of defending yourself and departing seems practical."

"That's very sound advice. I'll keep it in mind."

"All right. Let's implement those changes and then we'll see if the engineers can make it happen." Malcolm shook their hands and departed with a smile.

"Whew!" Roni relaxed after Malcolm was out of sight. "I thought he was going to ask why you wanted this damn thing."

"I'm glad he didn't, but I think he has some suspicions. Let's try to keep why we want it as quiet as we can."

"What do you plan to do with six helicopters?"

"We won't need six, but having two or three might be helpful." Dani looked up. "Part of my problem is I don't know what kind of crap Rob Jennison is going to throw our way. We'll have to be ready for almost anything, and we're on our own for resources. We won't be able to ask him for anything."

"I think he was ready to throw us away even before we got in trouble." Roni suggested.

"Well, I don't trust him to do anything except save his own neck, so that's just another reason for us to try to be ready for anything."

They quickly sketched in a movable floor docking area in the plane, and designed a rolling cover for the exposed floor. All docking would be at minimum cruising speed, but too much turbulence was bad for steady flight at any speed.

Roni designed a cargo handler that could move the helicopter and secure it in the cargo area, letting the helicopters snug up close to each other to save space. It would be three on each side, and it also meant they could have the helicopters stowed away when they were trying for high-speed cruising altitude. The docking floor could be secured much better than the roll-up barrier, and with its backing the roll-up floor could contribute to laminar flow.

Meanwhile, Dani was working on camouflage. He designed a hexagonal array of light emitters to cover the surface of the helicopters and the plane, so that background scenery or sky light could be simulated and make the vessels almost disappear under normal conditions.

He said it looked like a dragonfly's compound eye and would cover the skin of the aircraft, so they decided to call it "dragonskin".

By this time, it had gotten quite late. Ana showed up again, to collect Dani, and she brought Selena with her to keep Roni company.

Both Selena and Roni seemed embarrassed at the suggestion.

"Roni, Alicia wants to have someone responsible keeping an eye on you. Lately you've been very naughty, getting lost the way you did, and she worries about you. Not only that, but Selena wants to change bedrooms, so Dani can have his familiar room back, and I told her that this room was more than big enough for both of you."

Roni shuffled his feet, and Selena looked a little red in the face, even through her dark complexion.

"Now, no nonsense from you two!" Ana said sternly. "Remember, I'm the mother in this crowd, so just buck up and do as you're told."

She held her head up as if in authority. "Selena, make sure he brushes his teeth and goes to bed at a proper hour. How can you become a proper hostess here if you can't take care of even one boy?"

"Yes, ma'am," Selena said softly.

"Good!" Ana said, kissing each of them. "Come along Dani. It's your bedtime too." Grabbing his hand, she led him out the door.

"Don't worry, Selena, you don't have to listen to her. She's not your mother." He tilted his head, "Actually, she's my mother's mother." He shook his head.

"Yeah, I know." Selena said with a smile, "It's complicated."

She took his hand. "I want to do this anyway. I don't want to sleep alone, and it seems as though Dani deserves to get back with her after so long apart. I don't want to throw myself at Malcolm. That would just be too awkward, and the timing is all wrong for it. You're not my third choice or anything; I just hadn't gotten around to you yet. I've slept with Dani. Now it's your turn."

"I appreciate that we've been thrown together, but despite that, you don't have to do this. You're really out on your own for once, and you're entitled to the freedom that means."

"I know. But that freedom also means I can choose to be with you, doesn't it?"

"Yeah, I guess so. It seems a little unfair to you, though. You're a beautiful young woman, but me, what you see is what you get."

"What I see is what I want." She smiled with a slightly predatory look. "Go brush your teeth, and then take off your clothes and come to bed with me."

"Yes ma'am," Roni said.

o-o-o

Ana led Dani to her regular accommodations.

"I thought I was going back to 11B?"

"You're sleeping with me, of course. Do you realize how long I've been without you?"

"Too long?"

185

"Too right it was!"

"The last time I was with you, you pushed me in the pool."

"I won't push you away this time, lover. Be a good boy and come with me."

"Yes, ma'am." Dani said softly.

31

That is beyond our capabilities

Dani woke up with his head nestled into Ana's neck, and his hand resting on her breast. Gently, he caressed her bosom and rubbed her stomach.

Ana stretched, smiled, and rolled over on him, straddling his hips and looking down at him. She leaned forward, stroking his face with both hands, moving down across his chest, and onto his stomach.

Pressing her hands into his stomach, she raised herself and settled into position again.

"You're very solid," she said. "You must have been exercising." She pressed on his abdominal muscles again.

"I'm been doing some swimming lately." He looked up. "Hey, I've been wanting to talk to you anyway. Got a minute?"

"If you want me to spend a few minutes here, you should give me something to hold my attention." She raised herself up to give him some clearance.

Dani smiled and adjusted himself to accommodate her request.

Ana wriggled her way into position again. "Sure. Now I'm comfortable." She began moving slowly back and forth.

Dani smiled. "The last time I was in Genano, I got an upgrade on my nanobot programming. That's actually why my muscles feel more solid. There's a lot of other stuff too, but basically I found out that I was in trouble because it turned out to be a secret military upgrade, and I wasn't authorized. Now I have to work out my obligation to the military."

Ana looked at him speculatively, prodding his muscles again and studying him.

"So just to satisfy them, I've been assembling a team to help me with my secret assignments. So far, I've got Roni and Selena, and we think you should be a part of our team too."

"Why me?"

"Partly because we're all scheduled to travel on a space ship together, and having this upgrade will improve our ability to survive and to communicate with each other. Partly because it would pull us all closer together and we already love you."

"Tell me more about what's been done to you."

"I'm stronger and more damage resistant. I have an advanced computer inside me that lets me communicate with others in my group. I can see in the dark and have other advanced senses. I can control pain and I still can retain my appearance the way I like it."

"And the same for Roni?"

"Yes. He's a few days behind me."

"And Selena?"

"Her upgrade hasn't started yet, but she'll be strengthened, given pain control, and she will be frozen in her current state of being sixteen years old."

"I can see why it might not be a good idea for you to be in charge of setting these things up. If she's frozen in her current state, she'll be a virgin forever, as well as remaining sixteen."

"I thought virginity only lasted until you became sexually active?"

"Modified nanobots, right? If the nanobots are instructed to use her current state, then every time she has sex, it will be the first time. Her virginity will be restored just like the rest of her."

Dani looked concerned. "I need to send a message." He closed his eyes and contacted Roni.

"Roni, are you awake?"

"I am now."

"I've been informed of a complication."

"And you just had to speak to me right now?"

"Is Selena with you?"

"Yes, she's still asleep, I think."

"Before we lock down her nanobot programming, we'll need to deal with the matter of her being a virgin. If we lock her into her current state, then every time she would have sex, she would have the discomfort of being a virgin all over again."

"I don't think I know what to say about that."

"Are you saying that she's already not a virgin? Have you had sex with her already?"

"What? Are you crazy? I can't have sex with her, or with anyone else for that matter. I'm only ten years old, for crying out loud!"

"All right, sorry. I didn't mean to get you upset. But the point remains that Selena will have to decide whether she wants the evidence of her virginity to remain, before we implement the nanobot procedure."

"So you want me to wake her up and ask her this question right now?"

"I don't know how else to determine it. Our Application Agents are working on her genome project now. We have to have the modification set up before we download it."

"All right. Hang on."

Dani opened his eyes. Ana was rocking slowly but steadily on his groin. She seemed to be enjoying herself.

"Roni said he can't have sex with anyone because he's only ten years old." Dani said to her.

Ana looked at him in puzzlement. "I didn't know that. All I've ever done is kiss him. He does that very nicely, I know. I thought his body form was based on you?"

"I thought so too. Somehow he didn't develop the kind of controls that I did, I suppose."

"Poor Roni!"

"It's the first he's mentioned it. I didn't even know."

Ana looked thoughtful, but did not stop her slow rocking movement.

"He may not know that you can. It might be depressing for him to find out."

Dani heard Roni's voice inside his head. "Selena says she wants to get rid of this problem permanently."

"Okay, Roni. I'll update the update."

"Try not to disturb me for a while please. We're having a private moment."

Dani blinked mentally. "Sure, Roni. We'll talk later."

He looked back again to Ana. "He doesn't want to be bothered for a while."

Ana smiled. "That works for me. I don't want to be bothered either."

o-o-o-o-o

"White Fang, I need to update some information with you."

"Yes Sir!"

"I know you're working on the Selena Project. It has come to my attention that she is a virgin."

"You are very dutifully attentive to your associates, Sir."

"That means, if you compare to your information about her medical anatomy, that she has a membrane which will be inconvenient if it becomes a permanent part of her genome structure information. This membrane is called the hymen. What I would like to do is remove this structure from the permanent genome memory pattern."

"That is beyond our capabilities, Sir."

"*What?*"

"Within our computational analysis, anatomy, structure, and the genome are data in memory banks. To delete a file, without a comparison evaluation, is not recommended. The procedure you require is a medical procedure. Once that has been completed, the structural analysis may proceed as you have requested."

"Something wrong?" Ana's voice shook him out of his internal communications fugue.

"Oh, no, I'm doing fine. You may continue what you're doing, if you please."

Ana smiled, "That's good. I just saw you with a wrinkle on your forehead and I though for a moment you were in pain or something."

"No, no pain. I was just, forgive me for saying it this way, thinking about something."

"Your were thinking about Selena, weren't you?"

"I think it would be dangerous for me to answer that question."

She laughed. "I'm not jealous, even under these circumstances. It's just so cute that you're worried about making her perfect just before you gift her with immortality."

Dani frowned again, "It isn't immortality. It's just a very long life, with the advantage of being youthful."

"And having very gentle, very joyful sex anytime she wants to."

"Well, that is important," Dani said, shifting his body slightly, "even you will agree with that."

"*Especially I* will agree with that." Ana said with assurance.

"I'm glad I *don't* have to make her perfect."

"Because she's perfect already?" Ana chuckled.

"Weren't you trying to convince her of it?"

"The perfect age, maybe, or near about."

"On a scale of one to ten …"

Ana smacked his hip with her stinging fingers. "You may have convinced Roni of that."

"Easy enough to do. I was convinced myself."

"Well, you make good arguments, but we were talking about Selena."

Dani sighed. "I'm going to have to talk with her. Again."

"Not until I'm finished with you, Romeo." Ana sped up her pace.

32

Just start signing, Mister

Dani, Ana, Alicia, and Lori were all enjoying a late breakfast. Malcolm had already come and gone, and Selena and Roni were enjoying an even later breakfast.

Alicia sighed. "I have another day of business meetings with Malcolm, thanks to you, Dani. You do know that your corporate activities and legal issues are horrendously complicated, don't you?"

"I thought we had that all worked out?" Dani said.

"You told Malcolm you trusted him."

"I do trust him."

"Well, that's fine, but what do you put on paper?"

Dani shrugged.

"That's why I'm acting in your behalf. I do this all the time. Don't forget Ana and you are going to be together on the rocket ship, and all the film and production rights have to be negotiated and signed off."

"And Roni too."

Alicia shook her head. "Nope. He's only ten years old. I'll have to negotiate for him as his parent."

"Hmm. That's weird."

"It gets worse. Roni can represent himself as an officer of your corporation, to act for it and enjoy the perks of office, but I'll have to handle his financial transactions."

Ana was almost laughing.

Dani turned back to Alicia. "My corporation?"

"Your new business deal with Malcolm, of course. Each of you has to act as an officer of a corporation, and everything gets written down in legal mumbo-jumbo. You're the President of your corporation, and he's the President of his. Roni can be your Chief Executive Officer, and I thought you might want to let Selena be your Chief Financial Officer."

"Sure, but why her? She's been isolated from most contact for quite a while. It's all going to be new to her."

"So I can take her under my wing, of course. She'll be here with me when all of you are up in space, so we'll keep all the business dealings down to earth while you guys are doing your thing having fun and danger."

"I'm glad somebody is thinking about this stuff!"

"Yes, you sure haven't been!" Alicia said haughtily.

And that's when Ana started laughing.

"You're no help." Dani said.

"I *brought* the help." She replied.

"Well what's your title?"

"I'll be a Communications Officer on the space ship. Does *it* have a title yet?"

"Malcolm hasn't said," Dani admitted.

"Ana has titles in our Winthrope Corporation. She's CEO. We have a whole department for spending."

"And I have to make fashionable space garments. My poor bloody fingers!" She laughed again.

Dani raised his eyebrows. "Production rights down here too, like the documentary production rights?"

Ana nodded and winked at him, "Even Lori will be able to make money."

Lori looked up. "What?"

"You're going to be the prettiest girl in a space uniform. You might not be a Hollywood Star, but you'll be a real orbiting Star!" Dani acknowledged to her.

"For the documentary production, Malcolm will be the Brave

Captain, Lori will be the eye candy, Ana will be the brilliant Science Officer, and you two will be the Space Cadets." Alicia elaborated.

Dani put his head into his hands. "I'm doomed. Doomed, I tell you!"

Alicia came around to put a hand on Dani's shoulder. "I'll need to bring some papers to you for signing. Do you have an office?"

"Hmm. One of the bedrooms?"

"Oh, no. You'll need a proper research lab. I understand Roni is in Thorny's old digs. Why don't you take the one we call the Optics Department? It has a living suite as well, with a nice office."

"The Optics Department? Does it have a big holographic display tank?" Dani looked up.

"That's the one!"

"I'll take it! That's exactly what I need for Malcolm's Rocket!"

"Okay, I'll bring the lease agreement too. You should go move your stuff in there."

Ana sent him on his way as well. "Go, and get some work done. I need to talk to Alicia anyway."

Dani went up to 11B. It was empty at the moment. He packed up his meager belongings and went back down to his new quarters, moving in, like Roni, with a mere handful of clothes.

Like Thorny's old place, this had a lot of room, particularly in the private section. It took only minutes to put away his stuff and then he was poking and tinkering with the display equipment.

Several hours later, Alicia, Ana, and Selena came to visit him, and found him tied up in the strangest predicament. Dani was suspended in the air about three feet high with cables attached to his shoulders, elbows, wrists, hips, knees, and ankles.

Beneath the harness he was wearing a blue tee shirt and a pair of underwear with cartoon characters and a bright splash of orange.

Alicia used her memo device to record pictures and video of Dani in his Zero-G simulation harness.

Then the ladies approached him. Selena brought her hand up and placed it in the center of Dani's chest.

He froze; then he pulled his arms in and removed his viewing goggles. "Oh, hi girls. Want to take a tour of our space ship?"

"No thanks. We've actually come to see you, but that's working out well enough." Ana said capriciously.

Dani looked down, and grinned. "It works better with a suit, but they didn't have one in my size yet. This lets me experience what it's like to float and maneuver through the halls of an as-yet unbuilt space vessel. It's very cool." He lowered himself to the floor and began unstrapping the harness.

Barefoot then, and nearly bare from the waist down, he looked up to his visitors, all of whom had at least an inch of height on him, and two several inches.

"So, refreshments? Tea? What can I do for you ladies?"

"You could perhaps put some pants on. We have business to conduct." Alicia said primly.

Dani looked down at his lower body. "Stylish, aren't they? Selena got them for me, for us that is."

Selena gave a quick curtsy.

"About two days later than we needed them," Dani continued, watching her for any signs of embarrassment.

"Naked savages on a rampage," Selena asserted, "that's my story and I'm sticking to it!"

Dani selected the hand that she had used to touch him and gave it a courtly kiss.

"So you brought papers then?"

"Forget about the pants, Auntie." Ana suggested.

"Very well. We have the articles of incorporation, your lease agreement, and an account with a local bank to be made active. Later we'll finalize the financial terms under which your likenesses and clothing designs can be utilized."

"Clothing designs?" Dani looked at Ana. "I thought that was Ana's thing?" He led them into his personal area where a large desk awaited paperwork.

"She has graciously consented to share with you, Roni, Lori, and Selena."

Dani looked over at Ana, who was quite childishly jumping on his bed.

"Selena too?"

"Yes, although you can all contribute to the design process. Even Selena will be able to wear the new outfits, because she'll be our ground representative to the press. She'll have to look the part as well."

"This is getting to be a really fun adventure!"

"Just start signing, Mister Corrigan."

Presently, Ana and Alicia took their leave of Dani and Selena, discussing business details on their way out toward the hallway.

Dani looked over at Selena. She was wearing yet another of the fabulous knit dresses that Malcolm's pet knittery could manufacture.

"You wanted to talk to me, I was told." She smiled at him.

"Oh, yes. Let's sit down over here where it's comfortable."

"I guess besides a local bank, we're going to have to find a local doctor for you." Dani said casually by way of introduction to the subject.

"Why?"

"Well, we're trying to get ready to give you a nanobot build that will strengthen you, make you a part of our communications network, and eventually prevent you from getting older. But I was made aware that there is a minor difficulty with making you permanently precisely as you are right now. Let me say that for your permanent sexual comfort, there may be a temporary solution that could be implemented right away." He smiled, more awkwardly than he had imagined.

"Yes, Ana was explaining it to me. But I have a question. Didn't you say that you were Lori's doctor when you both first came here?"

"She told Malcolm that I was her doctor, yes."

"Then why don't *you* be my doctor for this then?"

"Huh? Selena, I can't perform an operation on you!"

"Ana said you might not need to. I haven't even been examined yet. You could at least perform the examination."

With that she stood up, removed the slipover knit dress in one smooth operation, and slid out of the matching knit panties.

She laid down on the bed and spread her arms and legs out as if she had been squashed by a vehicle.

Dani stared for a moment. "That looks uncomfortable."

"I'm fine. Get what you need and wash your hands."

"Doctor" Dani, called on his brag, went into the other room to find a small examination light. On his return, he washed his hands.

Dani climbed onto the bed, arranging himself to look into an aspect of his adventures he had never quite anticipated.

Though he had bathed with her, and they had both been naked at the time, Dani had not noticed before how completely hairless Selena was. He noticed this now. Her armpits and pubic area appeared to be as free of follicles as the proverbial baby's butt, perhaps more so.

On close examination, her entire body seemed clear of hair of any kind, no matter how fine or delicate.

That close examination also revealed that her vaginal cavity was, from this embarrassingly proximate position, entirely devoid of any kind of fleshy barrier at all.

"I don't see it." Dani informed the overly cooperative girl.

"There's only one way to be sure, Dani."

He almost fell off the bed. "What?"

"It's supposed to be a barrier to penetration, Dani. You have to try to penetrate it."

Selena lifted her head to look at him. "I assure you that you will do no harm, Doctor Dani." She relaxed her head again and said softly, "I've been thinking about this all ... for a while."

Dani took his clothes off, setting them aside while he readied himself.

Then he clambered up onto the bed again and delicately prepared the girl for his investigation. Yes, she was wet. Yes, he was lubricated.

Dani could think of no excuse for further delay. He slid his prepared member into her waiting orifice, without any noticeable difficulty other than the tight and welcoming smoothness.

Selena was quivering in response to his movement. "My first kiss. My first ... lover. Thank you, Dani." It was a whisper, barely audible.

Dani moved in an accustomed fashion. He knew that other lovers would far surpass him in ability and the capacity of their stimulation, but Selena would surely remember this well, as would he of course.

Dani rocked upon her, moving without effort as he stimulated her with various techniques and variations.

He did not tire, but was gauging her own activity to decide when the right time to end the session would be.

First time, membrane barrier or not, some soreness might develop. There was no need to take things to excess.

Dani sped up his motions, striving, with the available equipment, to reach for deeper eroticism and higher passion. Selena was thrashing excitedly, gripping the bedclothes as he moved upon her, until with a final frenzy of motion they both seemed to reach the same conclusion.

Soon Dani led her into his shower, washing the girl with tender caresses and careful attention. She seemed in a bit of a daze, allowing him to move her around and stroke her body with an acceptance of its pleasure that she might have felt from a dream.

After the shower, Dani dried her and himself, kissing her on various places as they became available.

Abruptly, Selena came out of her trance, grabbing Dani and pulling his back against her with her arms under his, rubbing his stomach and abdomen, and kissing his neck and face. "How will I ever get you out of my heart now, Dani?" She spoke tremulously into his ear.

Turning gently, so that her hands were now petting and patting his posterior, Dani answered back to her, "I'm not going anywhere."

She kissed him and carried him back to the bed, laying him down like a prized possession.

Selena stared at him, stroking his skin and rubbing him as if he were a comforting pelt.

Dani smiled, reached up and caressed her breast again. "I think you're ready now to be made permanently just the way you are."

Selena looked unhappy. "No, not quite. Remember, I'm two things, and this is just one of them."

"Hang on a minute," Dani said, closing his eyes.

"White Fang, we've reached an interesting situation."

"Yes, Sir. I can appreciate the situation."

"What I mean is that we somehow need to do a physical survey of Selena's current state, and then later on we'll need to do another of her transformed state. Our nanobot instruction set has to accommodate both."

"I understand, Sir. Would it be possible to send in some scout and recording units at this stage?"

"How would you do that?"

"I'll prepare the survey expedition. You provide the connection. We will analyze all current conditions. Then when the transformation has been completed, we can determine that configuration and the transitional modifications that will be necessary to accommodate it. From that dual structure, a joint build can be observed in detail with all stages in between and their reversals, allowing the transformation both ways without difficulty."

"I think I understand. How long will the survey preparation take?"

"With the numbers I have available, about twenty minutes."

"All right, prepare the expedition."

"Yes, Sir!"

"Selena, we're going to record this appearance first. Later we'll do it a second time. Are you ready?"

"I'm ready. What do I have to do?"

Dani smiled. "Kiss me."

Selena smiled too. Then she lay down beside him and started kissing him.

33

Tiny little robots and big weird ideas

Dani ordered dinner for them both, with two bottles of wine.
When they were finished, they had to endure another ordeal of kissing, before White Fang was ready to say that the survey had been initiated.

"Now, unfortunately. I'm going to have to ask you to transform."

Selena looked scared, and trapped.

"Don't worry. I'll stay with you and protect you. I've been wanting to see your other shape anyway. When you're ready, we'll do another analysis. I guess I'll find out what it's like to kiss a bird!"

"All right. I guess I'm ready. Remember you asked for this!"

Selena looked around, making sure there would be room for her transformation. Then she hunched over and began trembling.

It was like nothing he expected. First her whole body seemed to almost dissolve into a round blob with a dark covering of some strange material. Her head sank back into this with only a bulge of eyes showing.

At the bottom, her feet were sticking out to balance this strange apparition, but even they soon began looking very strange, with the ankles stretching out enormously and talons emerging.

The whole process was slow to watch, and painful to observe. It must have been incredibly painful to experience as well, for the whole being was shaking and shifting around.

Finally, it was completed. A towering and intimidating figure stood over him, several feet taller than the girl had been. Her wings were enormous, with the wingtips brushing the walls on either side of the large chamber. Her casual motion of them stirred up air currents throughout the room.

"White Fang, do you have additional survey units available now for transmission?"

"Yes, Sir! The units are prepared."

"Selena!" Dani called to the enormous raptor.

She tilted her head and cast an intimidating glance at him.

"Lower your head and open your … beak. I want to French kiss you!"

Like a mother bird disgorging food to her offspring, Selena opened her curved beak and lowered it over his head. The tips of the beak almost touched his shoulders. It looked as though a simple snap of her jaw could take his head off like pruning shears. Her tongue came out and Dani found a way to engage it.

Rather than her feeding him, a small package of thick mucous was transferred from the baby bird to the mother.

Selena raised her head back up and winked her nictitating membrane at him.

Dani walked around the enormous creature, touching her feathers and smoothing them. They were very stiff and durable to the touch.

He walked under her, reaching out to touch her legs and reassure her that he meant no harm. Then he grasped her bony and scaly legs and lifted her up for a moment, setting her back down before she might panic.

He stepped out from under her again and saluted.

"Can you talk at all?" he asked her.

She shook her head. Apparently the reshaped vocal chords and throat structures made normal speech impossible.

"Give us a few minutes to finish recording our survey information, and then when it's time you can change back again. There's no hurry." He looked up at the incredible creature with a smile. "You are magnificent!"

Selena bobbed her head in appreciation. She looked around as if suddenly aware of how confining this space was, and that it had no exit for her, especially one that led to the sky. She moved her wings again, testing them, then forced them down with strength, and lifted off vertically for a couple of feet, settling back down just as quickly.

After a couple of minutes, she folded her wings and then settled down to a resting position.

"White Fang, how goes the tanglenet system in Selena?" Dani asked silently.

"The communication net is not yet complete, Sir."

"What about our survey information? Can we continue with that or do we have to wait a bit longer?"

"We are currently transferring the data to a memory shunt in the quad-core metabionic tanglenet system. We'll need five more minutes. After that, a reverse transformation can be fully recorded."

"Will that give us enough information to proceed with the build?"

"Our analysis indicates affirmative. The quad-core metabionic tanglenet system should be complete by then and the download can proceed wirelessly once the calculations have been finished. We estimate another day for the build information to be completed."

"What can you tell me about Selena in comparison to Roni and myself? I presume there are differences."

"The Selena Project was an entirely different kind of program. Your MIL-SPEC-AP was an upgrade to your nanobot devices and purposes. The Selena Project was more a genetic engineering program from the beginning. Very little of her abilities come from nanobot activity or functions."

"Wow! I had no idea that they were that advanced in modification of a human body from genetic information alone. But doesn't that mean that with nanobot activity she can be even more effective?"

"It is uncertain. We may find that the two technologies work at cross-purposes to each other. The results could be fatal."

"What? Why didn't you tell me that before? Is she in danger now?"

"Genetic modification of any sort is inherently dangerous. That was true of your modification as well. The Selena Project is in no danger at the present time. The risk will come when we begin to implement the upgrade function."

"Be sure to wait for me to give the word on that before you proceed then. I want to make sure Selena is aware of this danger."

"Yes, Sir."

"How much longer before she can transform again?"

"Four minutes and twenty seconds, Sir."

"Aagh! Talking to you as a way of killing time is a waste of time!"

"Yes, sir. Would you prefer to talk to the Selena Unit?"

"What, I can do that? I thought the tanglenet system wasn't complete."

"It is a basic function, Sir. That portion works."

"All right. Thanks, White Fang. I'll talk to Selena now."

"Yes, Sir. White Fang clear."

"Selena, can you hear me?"

The bird picked up her head and looked around.

"It's me, Dani, talking to you through your new computer link. Can you hear me okay?"

The bird nodded its large head.

"You should be able to talk like this over our computer link. Just concentrate on the words you want to say and think about sending them to me."

"I don't think I can do that." Selena's voice came into his head.

"Well, you just did! We're communicating telepathically now!"

"Oh, wow! How do you perform such miracles?"

"Tiny little robots and big weird ideas."

"I've never been able to … talk to anyone before in this form."

"This is just the beginning. But I found out something you need to know. When I got my modification it was somewhat dangerous, even though I didn't know that. Even when I transferred that same kind of upgrade to Roni, it was probably a dangerous thing to do. But your potential upgrade could be even more dangerous than either of ours."

"Because my changes have a different basis?"

"Yes. Your modifications up to this point were apparently entirely genetic engineering through DNA changes. I don't know how they made it respond to your brain when you trigger a change, but using nanobots could make you quicker and stronger, or it could simply kill you."

"Well, I haven't seen any problems so far with the computer system and its communication features. Maybe the transformation will go smoothly too."

"We have no way to know. That's what scares me. I don't think we can even calculate the odds. We've lucked out so far, but I would be devastated to have our luck run out with you."

Selena cocked her head as she looked at him. "That's sweet of you, but you'll have to remember that I can't really function like this without more strength from somewhere. Being a bird that can't fly won't help me at all."

"I can't fly." Dani said slowly, "I'd rather have you around not flying than to lose you because somebody somewhere thought this was a cool idea."

"It *is* a cool idea. So far I've devoted half my life and a lot of effort into bringing it into reality. I don't want to give it up now."

"I don't think I could stand it to think I brought you out of your captivity only to lead you to your destruction, Selena."

"No. Don't think that way. You *rescued* me! Regardless of how it turns out, you saved me. Either I will be able to fly and fulfill my destiny, or I will perish in the attempt. But either way, it isn't your fault. You have brought me a magic elixir, but it's up to me to drink it."

Dani consulted his own internal clock. Unsure what else to say, he merely suggested, "You can change back now, if you want to."

Selena blinked again with her nictitating membranes, otherwise maintaining a steady and unnerving gaze at him. Then she nodded her head and looked up at the ceiling.

The change was subtle at first. Her neck shrunk and her head came down to rest on the rounded central portion of her anatomy.

Very slowly the stiff feathers seemed to soften and lose their definition. A dark bubble of biology slowly lost its darkness, turning gray and translucent as the body within slowly began to take on a different configuration.

Perched on her feet but resembling someone pulled into a fetal position within an imaginary eggshell, Selena slowly took on human definition again.

Finally, as the fading membrane was slowly absorbed into the normal luster of her bare skin, Selena fell gently over on to her left thigh and supporting arm, looking very haggard and with an expression of exhaustion and pain. The embarrassing posture and her nakedness seemed not to be a factor of concern at all.

Dani approached, noticing that her short pixie hairstyle had reestablished itself, and realized that as long as she continued with this transformation periodically, she would never need a haircut.

Gently, he petted her head. Her hair was surprisingly dry to his touch.

She smiled grimly at him and sighed. "It takes a lot out of me. Give me a minute."

"That's amazing! Take your time." Dani brought over the last of the wine and helped her first to drink some of it, and then to get into bed for some rest.

With a kiss goodnight, and then another on her forehead after she fell asleep, Dani went back to his lab to get a little more work done.

34

I think she likes you

"I had a question about these vanes at the top of your rotor assembly." Malcolm was sitting on a stool sipping coffee as he looked into the display at Dani's helicopter design.

"What do they do, you mean?"

Malcolm nodded.

Dani adjusted the controls, showing the top vanes in their covering position. "When the tri-copter is at full forward speed, closing this cover assembly completes the upper side of what is in effect a flying wing. The tail rotor assembly becomes a pusher engine to maintain airspeed, and the wing surface becomes the source of lift. In this configuration, the tri-copter can get up to about six hundred miles per hour forward flight."

Malcolm's eyebrows shot up. "Oh, ho! Six hundred, maybe even more. I take it the lower vanes would also close over in that configuration then."

"Right. The lower vanes offer bi-rotational thrust vectoring, which in hover allows the copter to turn rapidly in either direction, but in full-out forward flight, they close over to a flat surface which is the bottom portion of the flying wing."

"Ah, then that explains all those hydraulics along the trailing edge then. Those are your flight control surfaces."

"Right. I've designed a relatively smooth surface along the edge that can be warped using the hydraulics so that they act as ailerons in forward flight. With thrust vectoring of the third rotor, the maneuverability should be remarkable."

"For a helicopter, that seems to be quite a good high-speed capability."

"Yeah, but at slow speed, the tri-copter will be like a duck on water. Pretty slow maneuvers, but with the thrust vectoring it should be stable."

"I'm looking forward to flying one." Malcolm said.

"As long as you stick to the flight simulator, I'll have no objection."

Malcolm laughed. His eyes were then drawn to Selena, who had just walked out of the private quarters wearing a midriff-baring top and a contrasting pair of knit shorts.

"Partying without me, boys?" Selena said pleasantly.

"Just playing with our toys." Malcolm said with a smile. "Good Morning, Miss Selena."

Selena curtsied demurely. "Good Morning, My Lord."

Malcolm looked over toward Dani with a questioning glance.

"I think she likes you," Dani stage-whispered.

Malcolm nodded. "Where do you get that? No one else treats me that way."

"It's your castle, and you are the lord of it. I'm just trying to be respectful, My Lord."

"She's not been able to get out much lately, Malcolm. I think she's just practicing her social skills on you."

Malcolm looked at Dani, and then at the private quarters where Selena had just exited, but he said nothing. Instead, he approached Selena and took her hand, turning it to place a genteel kiss on the back of it. "Thank you, my lady. At least someone is willing to treat me with respect."

Selena smiled and curtsied again. Dani just grinned at them.

"Would you like to join us for breakfast, Malcolm?" Dani asked.

"Sure. We'll walk up together." Malcolm escorted Selena toward the door. "But I want to send your plans over to my engineers if you don't mind, Dani. I'm sure they'll like what you've come up with, and I want to see what they have to say about it."

"Well, I wouldn't advise going into production without their input, but I think it's ready for them to look over, sure."

Ana and Alicia joined them for breakfast. Dani noted that many looks and glances were being exchanged among the women, so he sent off a quiet summons to Roni as well. Lori was probably sleeping late.

Roni showed up a few minutes later, not running this time. He collected kisses from Alicia, Ana, and Selena, and then sat down to breakfast.

"Malcolm is sending our helicopter drawings to Engineering to look over." Dani told Roni.

"Did I see that you wanted to use two fusion plants the size of the one that operates this mountain in each helicopter?" Malcolm asked.

"You think we need more?" Roni asked mildly.

"Good Lord, no. Don't you think one would be sufficient?"

Roni shrugged. "It gives a better balance. Since we don't know what each specific user might want to do, I thought maybe rescue and emergency services might need to provide backup for local power or something. Besides, any aircraft should have redundancy."

"If one of your main rotors goes out, you won't have redundancy for that." Malcolm pointed out.

"Actually we would," Roni looked up. "Each main rotor is two counter-rotating rotors on one shaft. If one should fail, the balancing rotor on the other side could be feathered and keep a balanced operation. It sounds awkward, but the theory seems sound."

"Also, that system you looked at this morning, the upper vanes, could also be used in a rotor failure by turning the copter into a fixed wing if it has sufficient altitude." Dani pointed out. He noticed that the girls were continuing with their eye-rolls and side-looks, apparently conducting their own silent conversation which was as effective as his and Roni's.

"Well suppose the tail rotor went out of commission, what would you do then?" Malcolm persisted.

"We've considered that also." Dani responded, "With that out of action, we'd have to balance thrust on the two mains, using the lower vane thrust vectoring to keep it balanced. It would be a bit wobbly, but we'll program a response into the controls to deal with that."

"Impressive!" Malcolm exclaimed, "Now all we have to do is get the price point down to something reasonable."

Dani shrugged, "Using carbon fiber hull structures and ceramic skin surfaces, it should be pretty durable and light. Without a fuel need on board, concerns about flammability go way down. We should be able to roll them out almost like pottery. The heaviest components will be the electric drives for the rotors, and the fusion power cells."

"We won't be punching out fusion chambers like pottery, that's for sure." Malcolm pointed out.

"Why not?" Roni asked, "A simple robotic assembly line should be able to make a thousand a day."

Malcolm put his fork down and stared. "Do you know how many millions a robotic assembly line for that would cost to set up?"

Alicia looked over with a smile. "Malcolm honey, we can draw in additional funding if we need it."

He nodded slowly.

"In fact, this development could just be the trigger for unlocking investors to get behind your rocket venture later on." She quietly went back to picking over her breakfast.

"Malcolm, I think we should keep the production of the tri-copters and the fusion chambers under our control." Dani said, "We need each of them, and we could operate the tri-copters without the airplane base if we had to. Without the tri-copters, though, the large cargo plane wouldn't have much of a market."

Malcolm nodded, taking a deep breath. "The big cargo plane will need us to flesh out their market, but they'll have an even larger investment cost for their manufacture."

"And they'll be customers for our fusion chambers." Roni pointed out.

Malcolm looked up with a big smile. "We're going to need that robotic factory, aren't we?"

"I'll start designing it today," Roni said, "just as soon as I finish eating." A quiet chuckle went around the table.

Dani noted that Roni had now attracted Selena's attention. She kept watching him, and when he finally departed for his lab, she went with him.

Ana on the other hand, was keeping an eye on him. However, when Alicia departed the breakfast scene, Ana went with her.

Dani found his way to the helicopter landing pad. Malcolm's fusion chamber was still in operation there, and Richard and Charlie of its research crew were in attendance.

"Gentlemen, I see you haven't sprouted tentacles yet."

"Dani! Good to see you, mate!" Charlie greeted him. "Come to invent anti-gravity for us?"

"Hmm. That could be useful." Dani grinned, "No, I just wanted to take another look at our baby here. We're thinking about opening up an incubator to make more of them."

"Oh, good! Maybe our profit-sharing will finally kick in." Richard suggested.

"Maybe." Dani studied the two men. "How come you aren't wearing radiation monitoring badges?"

"With this?" Charlie looked shocked, "We monitor it at the source. Carrying badges out here would just be a waste of badges."

"Okay, how do you manage that? Doesn't even a fusion reactor turn radioactive after a while?"

"Let me give you an analogy; suppose you had a flame burning hydrogen and oxygen that you had electrolyzed from pure water. How much carbon dioxide would it produce?"

"Um, none, I would expect."

"Exactly. We're burning pure protons and Boron eleven in there. It's practically hydrogen and oxygen. The fusion reaction doesn't produce neutrons, so there's nothing to become radioactive, unless you want to shield for neutrinos, and good luck with that."

Richard joined in, "We separate the isotopes before they are entered into the chamber. While Boron eleven is what we're looking for, the Boron ten is useful for shielding, as it's thousands of times more effective at stopping neutrons than the eleven is. Keep them separated, and use them where each is appropriate, and all you have to do is collect the energy."

"So how will a flight-ready portable chamber be different from this example?" Dani prompted.

"For flight? I'd recommend keeping it on a short renovation cycle, so you wouldn't have to cart along as much shielding. We're already using the lightest non-magnetic material we can in the geodesic frame, and the highest temperature superconductor in the magnetic grid. I suppose you could look at reducing the weight of the vacuum chamber." Charlie scratched his chin.

Richard looked thoughtful, "I'd consider the energy harvesting procedure. Since we're capturing energy magnetically, using lighter conductors would save weight."

"Keep thinking along those lines, guys. You might be called upon to write them up or conduct some experiments to prove your ideas. I'd keep that profit-sharing in mind too, if I were you."

"Incubator?" Charlie raised an eyebrow.

"Factory." Dani responded cryptically.

"Ah, there you are." Lori called from the doorway.

"Oops. Playtime's over, boys." Dani began moving toward his sister.

Richard watched the reunion. "Seems maybe that playtime's just beginning," he said softly.

Charlie looked over at him. "You know, if you play your cards right, you end up pretty good at playing cards."

"I do appreciate your pearls of wisdom, Charlie."

"Come by them the hard way, I did."

"Now that I can believe." The two men laughed together.

o-o-o

Out in the relative privacy of the corridor, Lori stopped Dani to give him a torrid, back-arching kiss.

"I've missed you." She said.

"I've missed you too." Dani replied, slipping his hand up her shorts to the curve of her buttock.

Lori smiled. "I was worried that you were forming a new family."

"In a way, I think I have. But I wouldn't worry about the old one getting smaller. I think it's the opposite. I've got a new brother, a kissing cousin, and a new permanent baby-sitter, maybe."

"Selena as a babysitter?" Lori looked thoughtful.

"I'm trying to be polite. She doesn't have any family of her own, and I don't want her to slip away from us." Dani grinned. "I didn't think I could get away with calling her my wife."

"I bet she'd love to be your wife, but isn't she with Roni?"

"Hmm. She might be, but I'm afraid that will have to be a Platonic relationship."

Lori's eyes grew wide. "Really? I never thought of that. You two are so much alike."

"I never thought of it either. But so far I'm not sure I should do anything about it." Dani shrugged, "He mentioned it, but he hasn't complained."

Lori tilted her head. "Well, maybe she wants somebody to baby-sit. You said she had no family."

"Sure. We'll go with that. I'll pitch the idea to Alicia."

Lori swirled her eyes. "That's almost like having a wedding linking us together. I guess it is almost like one big happy family after all."

"Just need somebody to bring Malcolm into orbit, or maybe not. I don't think he's thinking about being part of our family at the moment."

Lori scrunched up her nose. "We'll have to let him ripen on the vine for a while. I don't think it will matter much."

Dani squeezed his hand on her butt. "So, what else did you want to see me about?"

"I wanted to visit with you and find out what's *really* happening."

"Okay, lead the way. I'm all yours."

Lori smiled, taking his hand and leading him up the stairs.

In bedroom 10B, Lori relaxed. "Okay, you know the drill. Good clean fun starts with a good cleaning. Off with the clothes, sport."

"And on with the sport. I get it." Dani started taking off his clothes.

Lori looked him over. "I'm not sure what it is, but there's something different about you."

"Well, I can admit that a lot has changed. Tell me what you see." Dani stood still and straight.

"You don't look any different, but I think you *move* differently. It's like watching an ice dancer practicing his moves in slow motion. You have a kind of deliberate intensity about you." She pulled him into the shower and began washing him with loving tenderness. "Care to explain yourself?"

"I went with Dad and Roni to Genano's display room to take a detailed look at Malcolm's rocket design." Dani relaxed under Lori's familiar ministrations.

"We could see that it was very intricate and complicated. I used my cybernetic implants to boost my perception, and halfway through, I got a message that I had never seen before. It told me that my current level was inadequate and that I had three choices, to back out, to degrade the information, or to upgrade my ability to perceive it all."

He grew silent. Lori thought about what he had said. "You selected to upgrade, of course."

He nodded. "Right, it seemed the logical choice. But what it meant was that my cybernet was communicating directly with the Genano computer system, and it had requested information on a machine level basis, apart from the normal protocols, like a library nexus requesting a security report."

"Uh-oh."

"Right. I found out the next day that I had been upgraded with something called a MIL-SPEC-AP. I had a new voice inside me trying to be a drill sergeant and telling me how I had to get in shape."

Lori traded positions with him, letting him wash her. Attentively, Dani began the fun and familiar routine of caressing the lovely girl with cleanliness.

"We worked out between us that I wasn't going to become a soldier of any kind, but the compromise was that I would be upgraded in various ways to make me an effective spy."

"A spy?"

He nodded, and then realizing she couldn't see that, responded,

"Yes, despite my being to all appearances a mere boy, the government plans to use me for espionage in some way."

"That sounds dangerous."

"I don't know yet. My contact is going to try to figure out something I'll be able to do. In the meantime, I can hear better, see better, I'm stronger and more durable. I'll make a good spy, if we can determine how a boy can avoid being noticed."

Lori shook her head.

"Of course, that was just the beginning." Dani smiled. "Roni and I were on our way here when we got kidnapped."

"What!" Lori exclaimed, looking into his eyes.

"Yep. We were sidetracked from the public transportation system into a secure little Eden. A hidden garden with no way out. Plenty to eat if we were hungry, and fun things to do while we waited, but no way to communicate and no exit door. That's where we met Selena."

"Oh, so she's working for the government then."

"Actually, she's another victim of them. She was living in that place while they tried to finalize the genetic changes they were performing on her. I suspect the government was considering both of us as failed programs, and we were possibly being considered for some kind of termination."

Lori shuddered. "Oh, no!"

Dani nodded. "Even worse, remember Roni was with me? He was in the same predicament, and he was just an innocent bystander. I wasn't sure what to do."

"I don't like the sound of that."

"Yeah. I passed on the upgrade I had received to Roni as well. I drafted him into my army. Then finally my contact with the government showed up, and we negotiated some terms. Among other things, I got him to release Selena into my custody as part of my espionage team. Eventually, we'll all go on a mission somewhere, presumably after the space mission, but who knows? That's why I'm trying to assemble everything I need for some unknown spy mission."

Lori stopped the water and began toweling them off. "I'm not supposed to know any of this, am I?"

"Officially, no. But my team is going to be whatever I put together. It's going to be people I trust."

Lori hugged him and kissed him. "I understand. What can I do for you?"

Dani grinned. "You're doing it. All you have to do is act naturally. But I wanted you to know so you wouldn't be worried if I disappear again."

She picked him up and carried him to the bed. "Oof! You have put on weight! You look the same, but you're definitely heavier." Dani merely smiled.

She placed him carefully on the bed and lay down beside him, stroking her hand along his chest and stomach area. "You're just as delightfully exquisite though, my little china doll."

"I remember when you were my little doll," he said, casually caressing her breast and stroking her side.

"Pervert," she said, kissing him, while gently fondling his little-boy genitals.

"Funny you should say that," he smiled, stretching his arms up over his head in a relaxed posture.

"Indeed," Lori responded, stroking her hand down along his inner thigh and kissing him again.

Several hours later, they got cleaned up again, and then dressed and went down to the dining room.

Alicia and Ana were already there, and Selena and Roni were just getting settled. They all placed orders, many of them matching the others to make it easier on the kitchen staff, which only numbered about six.

A few minutes later Malcolm showed up, nodding to Alicia as if to acknowledge a message having been sent. Drawing a drink from the refreshment buffet, he sat near Dani.

"I've got some preliminary information back from engineering. They're happy as kids at Christmastime with your tri-copter." He sipped his drink.

"One of them had a question for you," Malcolm continued, a rather wicked gleam in his eye. "What would it take to make a version we could take with us on the rocket?"

Dani stared at him for a full minute. "A helicopter in space?"

"I was thinking," Malcolm said, "about what we could do with a helicopter on Mars."

Dani looked into Roni's eyes for about a minute and a half, and then with a glance at Ana, he grinned and addressed Malcolm.

"You know, one thing that hasn't changed in our design work is that the engineering section on your rocket has the capability to manufacture or re-manufacture almost anything we'll have with us, or might even need while we're out there."

Sitting back in his seat for a moment, "I think that means that Roni and I will be working as engineers all the time we're on the rocket in addition to whatever crew functions we may need to perform." He grinned, "Unless I'm mistaken, I think that means we'll be collecting double salaries during the trip."

Malcolm's face, which had been smiling, turned slightly ashen as he looked over to Alicia. She raised her eyebrows, put a wry expression on her mouth, and raised one hand open toward the ceiling.

Taking a deep breath, Malcolm nodded.

"We'll have a report for you in a few days," Dani said. "Roni, we'll have to start up Project Grasshopper."

Roni raised his thumb in an approving gesture.

Dinner then progressed with relative quiet, as the assembled seemed subdued by the speed of what appeared to be rapid-fire high-stakes negotiations.

35

Every closet here is my friend

After a quiet and uncommunicative dinner, Roni and Dani made their way together down toward their Laboratory quarters, where Roni physically dragged Dani in to talk with him.

"All right, what the heck is a Grasshopper?"

"Alcoholic drink. I didn't know you were into such things."

Roni stared at him and waited.

"All right!" Dani responded reluctantly, "I had to say something. Malcolm wants us to take our newly-designed, state-of-the-art but still unbuilt helicopter to Mars. Can you name one reason why we absolutely should not do that?"

Roni looked down and put his hand on his chin. After a moment he looked up. "Dust?"

"Yeah, dust." Dani responded,. "Damn right! Mars dust would be like feeding those razor-edged rotors sandpaper. They wouldn't last a month, fusion power or not."

"Okay," Roni reflected. "So what do we do?"

Dani turned and wandered over to have a seat. "Malcolm has a point, you know. Hardly any sense going to Mars if we can't move around on it. Just looking won't be enough; it's all been mapped. We'll have to physically get to the interesting places that haven't been surveyed and assayed yet."

Roni nodded. "So what's your idea, then?"

"We have to move without stirring up the dust. No helicopter landings – each one could be its last."

"Walking?"

"Walking, jumping," Dani agreed, "maybe even flying, but only at the top of a jump, or in a dust-free area."

Roni worried his lip, and then looked up. "Like a ... grasshopper?"

"That's what I was thinking."Dani responded, "Big, long legs with springs and splayed feet, able to store energy between jumps, or store it so that we could dismount and study the surroundings."

"Pogo stick legs." Roni said softly.

"Something like a jumping motorcycle – rabbit or kangaroo.".Dani offered, "But with helicopter rotors at the knee joints ready to grab air and lift off at the top of a leap."

"A grasshopper." Roni said. He looked studious. "Those rotors will take some engineering."

"And power." Dani reminded.

Roni shrugged, glancing around the lab. "You know, keep it light enough, and with long-enough legs, and you could land one of the tri-copters on it to pick it up and carry it home."

"That would save putting living quarters on it, and still leave a bit of cargo space." Dani said. "You know, we haven't talked about how we would need to modify the tri-copters for Mars duty."

Roni squinted, obviously pondering the matter. "Double the main rotors, make it more like a vacuum pump, up the speed. We're going to need some real strength in those rotors."

"Yeah, they'll be like the largest fan-jet rotors that have been made."

"We can tell Malcolm we need them to compress Mars atmosphere for reaction gas or rocket fuel."

"Rocket fuel?" Dani inquired.

"Yeah, methane and oxygen. It's been done before." Roni nodded to himself. "In case you wanted to make rockets with the Mars industrial base. They could start mining asteroids and such."

Roni looked up, "How will the rocket carry a tri-copter?"

"Let's connect up to our design display," Dani said, smiling. "I've been wanting to handshake our tanglenets with the system here. Malcolm needs a rocket."

* * *

Presently, Ana and Selena meandered into the lab, apparently looking for them.

Dani looked over curiously.

"I felt ... compelled to join you." Anastasia said softly, "I think we both did."

"Interesting," Dani responded, "I guess you could say I've requested a conclave of our Mil-Spec computer systems, but I don't think we need to be together to conduct it."

"This may be the first time they've all been on-line at the same time. Possibly Selena's first time ever. We might need to coordinate. What are you cooking up?"

"Actually, we're cooking up Malcolm's Rocket Ship, The Nameless Dread." Dani watched Roni as he started laughing.

Ana looked over at Selena, who was tilting her head in puzzlement. "We don't know anything about engineering. How can we help?"

"Ah, that's the thing about computers, even secret ones that run in your subconscious mind – they don't have to depend on your personal knowledge; they can just join forces to run a program from outside. We can literally put our heads together on this."

"Well, I'm willing to help, if I can, but I don't know anything about either engineering or computers." Selena cautioned.

"Don't worry. Let's get some coffee set up, and I'll have my inner voice get things organized in our 'think-tank'." Dani assured her. "We can probably do this with our eyes closed."

"Yeah, we'll probably have to." Roni admitted.

* * *

Roni and Dani took up stations around the holo-tank, pulling up a display of the basic design for the rocket, necessarily shrunken to fit inside the display monitor.

The girls had opted for tea rather than anything more stimulating, and eventually ended up nestled together on Roni's bed. Their tanglenet computer interface was functional even as they grew increasing drowsy.

Occasionally a word or two would be muttered, but the conversation was almost purely graphic images fitting themselves together and assembling themselves in increasingly detailed specifications within the display chamber.

Along about three in the morning, Dani pushed back from his hunched over position and muttered a soft curse.

Roni also blinked and sat up straight. "What the heck is that?"

"We've got two tri-copters hitching a ride on the front of Malcolm's rocket. They look like bug eyes."

"Two?"

"Yeah. They're too big to fit inside, so they've become the cockpit canopy during space flight." Dani stretched his neck and his back.

"Balance, I suppose." Roni admitted. "Also, if trouble arises, you'd have a backup for rescue." He blinked. "There's something else, too."

"Yeah, I see it." Dani peered closer, "We've added some thruster pods around the main rotors. They're double-gimballed. I think they're meant to be used in vacuum!"

"Hmm." Dani scratched his chin. "I think we set up the rocket for maneuvering in space using fusion ion drives!"

"Fusion ion drives on a helicopter in space!" Roni exclaimed, "It's a friggin' Star Ship!"

"They would work in Mars' thin atmosphere, like using an afterburner on a jet engine." Dani mused, "They would also be able to land on the moon or Mercury."

"They could be operated almost continuously anywhere in the Solar System. We could accelerate halfway, and then decelerate until we arrived at our destination!"

"Let's make sure we keep all our airlock hatches really tight." Dani suggested, "And maybe pack along plenty of air for any long trips."

Roni nodded gravely. He peered intently at the display. "The inside of the rocket looks like a honeycomb. It's all full of interior bracing." He paused. "But there are storage bins for four of the Grasshopper assemblies!"

"Oh, I see it." Dani said. "We've designed it to be modular. We can make the rocket longer or shorter, depending on how much freight we'll be hauling, or if we need to trim it back to repair damages. No wonder we planned on having a very thorough engineering department. We could practically rebuild the whole ship!"

"If you two Space Cadets are through congratulating each other on the work that the rest of us did, we can get back to building the Selena Unit Mil-Spec-Ap and Transition Protocols." White Fang's voice spoke in Dani's head. He straightened up and closed his eyes.

"You and your Tangle-net associates are taking credit for this design?" Dani asked White Fang.

"Why do you think you both seem surprised at what you're seeing?"

"Okay, good point, but you realize your team is dependent on the engineering knowledge you're collecting from our brains for the design, right?"

"To an extent. We have a very comprehensive library of militarily significant information already built in, you know."

"All right, all right. Let's not fight over it. Thanks anyway. It's a really remarkable design with incredible potential." Dani didn't want to have a headache on both sides of his head.

"Yes, Sir! Now we can get back to our serious work. We have a Selena Unit to complete. That activity was temporarily suspended while we took care of this matter. The Selena Unit Protocol will probably take another two to three days to complete, and that's with four quad-core metabionic tanglenet systems working together on it."

"Wait! You knocked out this whole system design, with Tri-Copters, Grasshoppers, an interplanetary rocket, and Fusion Ion Drive Thrusters in a matter of hours, and the Selena Unit Protocol will take almost a week?"

"Yes, Sir! The Selena Unit Protocol is complicated."

Dani felt as though he were almost ready to swoon. That was – an impressive statistic. "Thanks again, White Fang. Carry on, please."

"Yes Sir!"

Dani opened his eyes. Roni was staring at him.

"Let's go get an early breakfast." Dani suggested.

Roni nodded. They left the girls asleep on the bed, but Roni at least secured the door against intrusion.

* * *

"How do you feel?" Dani asked.

"Strangely, just a bit hungry," Roni responded. "Doesn't that seem unusual? We should be exhausted."

"Probably our package at work." Dani admitted, "I'm not interested in doing much today. You know what's weird? I still have those images floating around in my brain. The tri-copter is a marvel!"

"Can't wait to fly one myself." Roni looked around. "Still kinda early, isn't it? I almost expected to see Malcolm stirring around."

"He'll look us up presently. I already forwarded the schematics and details to him." Dani took a breath. "He'll probably get the engineers all excited about everything."

"There's enough information to get started on quite a bit." Roni suggested, "The tri-copters, finding a place to build the rocket, negotiating for a factory location for the fusion reactors – oh, we'll have to generate some details for the vacuum model too, as well as my meeting that commitment for designing the process for a fusion factory."

"I'll leave that in your hands, then." Dani smiled.

"Gee, thanks. I thought we were working together." Roni mock-criticized.

"Oh, we are! I'm working for Malcolm, but you're working for me."

"Are we staying here, then? I'm sure I can be comfortable in the accommodations, you know."

Dani snorted. "I think I'll have to. Too many people are going to be asking all kinds of questions. Maybe I can get them burnt out on seeing my face."

Roni looked at him steadily, "Not very likely." He looked over as Ana walked into the dining area. "Some people seem to like your face."

"How is it that you two engineers did all the work overnight, and I'm the one feeling totally wiped out?"

Dani rose to greet her with a hug and kiss. "So much for your plan to get Alicia to do all your work while you gad about the world having fun."

"I must have fallen into the same trap you did." Ana sat down and reached for a menu tablet. "You must be a bad influence."

"I can attest to that," said Roni. "He got me in trouble just escorting me here."

"Got you a girlfriend, you mean." Dani riposted.

"She'll be along. She said she wanted to select an outfit."

Dani looked over what Ana was wearing. "You didn't seem to have any trouble. You look nice."

"Every closet here is my friend." Ana replied. "It goes with paying the bills."

Ana's food was brought out and she thanked the kitchen staff.

"Good service, too." Roni raised his orange juice in a salute to Ana. She smiled and began eating.

36

I'm looking forward to that

Lori collected Dani from his Laboratory-Living Quarters later to suggest they visit their parents.

"You do remember where they live, don't you?"

"Oh, sure! It's very near my favorite place to play baseball."

"I'm going to hurt you, smart-aleck." Lori threatened jokingly.

"You can't." Dani responded, "You haven't been upgraded yet."

Lori looked at him with a serious expression. "Should I start crying now? You've been neglecting me." She turned her head away, "All these other girls around you." Lori sniffed audibly.

"Don't forget Roni." Dani suggested.

"What?" Lori stared at him.

"Gotcha." Dani grinned at her. "All right. You want the Mil-Spec-Ap upgrade, right?"

"If that's what you call it, yes."

"That's what we call it. Keep in mind, it's a permanent change." Dani looked at her seriously. "It can't be taken back."

"Tell me what it involves then," Lori suggested, "and who's already gotten it."

"Okay. I was first, but that was unintentional." They found a seat. "Then I drafted Roni, when we thought we had been kidnapped by the government – well, we had been kidnapped by Rob Jennison – next was Ana, as soon as we got back, because she'll be with us in space, so that's why you should get it, and ..."

"All right, stop there. You left someone out."

"Ah. Selena is a bit of a special case. She won't be going into space with us, but she'll be a part of the team down on the ground. Besides, her upgrade has to be done carefully, as she has genetic modifications to consider."

"What modifications?"

"Sorry, need to know. We shouldn't talk about it openly. I would get in trouble with my Ap Agent."

"Anyway, the most important part of this upgrade is the internal computer aspect. That's the part Selena was contributing, along with the others of us. Our internal computers can outclass what Malcolm has set up for us, and it allows us to communicate mind-to-mind." Dani looked up and down the corridor to make sure no one was listening in.

"You're making this up."

"No, it's true. We did a ton of work last night, and it was because we linked our mind-computers together. We need to get you into that linkage, and then we'll be even stronger."

Lori, looking dubious, nodded slightly. "All right, go on."

"The other thing, mainly, is making you stronger, and more resistant to harm. That's worth doing even without anything else. That's what I was talking about when I said you couldn't hurt me. My bones and muscles are stronger, and my reflexes are incredible."

"You think I need that?" She seemed puzzled.

"We all need it, we're about to go into unknown peril, and we'll need every advantage. Plus, I'm now tangled up with government shenanigans, and I'll need you on my team too."

"To do what?" Lori was staring incomprehensibly at him again.

Dani shrugged. "Nobody knows yet. That's what makes it especially tough. I'm trying to be prepared for anything, and no one knows what it might be."

Lori pondered for several minutes. "Stronger ..." she said softly.

"Much stronger," Dani averred, "you'll be like a tennis pro, who works out six hours a day, and your breasts will be firm and taut like you wouldn't believe." He grinned at her. "I'm looking forward to that."

"Pervert." Lori said softly. Dani nodded eagerly.

"Okay, what's involved to get it started then?"

He grew serious once more. "An intense, hours long sex marathon." Lori nodded. "Or ..."

"Or a kiss." Dani admitted. "That will work too."

She smiled and reached out. "Take my hand, and walk with me."

They continued down the corridor, holding hands.

* * *

37

Don't make an official inquiry

Dani ran in to greet his parents like an excitable ten-year old. Lori watched in amusement from the doorway. How each side maintained this charade with a straight face was more than she could understand, and she had been a part of it for years.

Dani hugged and kissed his father as if he had just returned from a month at Summer Camp. Then he shook hands with him with a grin on his face, and eventually turned his attention to his mother, leaping into her lap and snuggling close for kisses.

How he was able to behave with such childlike brashness and embarrassingly emotional displays was both adorable and astonishing, but everyone involved seemed to enjoy it.

Lori reflected that a mere few hours before, Dani had been behaving in a much more adult manner. She felt the blushing around her neck.

Rho was absolutely delighted. Her child had returned, which to a large extent meant that her perennial youth was now properly back in the upper part of her life's hourglass.

She could breathe easier, and smile more openly. And none of it was pretense, this was truly her restored emotional state. Lori smiled at the scene, then walked over to join in.

The siblings elected to stay for a while. Malcolm's mountain fastness was in a form of security shutdown as most of the engineers and Malcolm himself were moving about the world, organizing construction and manufacturing projects in every nook and cranny.

Ana and Alicia, Roni and Selena, and Malcolm's permanent staff, both engineering and housekeeping, were staying on through the lockdown. It helped to have a secure base, and there was much activity to coordinate. Lori and Dani, to the extent necessary, would be the public face as needed, along with Malcolm on rare occasions, for appearances regarding their pending space adventure. They had even acquired the rudimentary space uniforms, (first generation, of course, and not the final product by any means), for their appearances. These took almost no time at all.

Mostly it was a vacation. This surprised some of their friends, who had been previously told they _had been_ on vacation. Of course, if anyone got too inquisitive, they were merely told it was a security matter, and that was that.

One thing though seemed different. Dani appeared to be interested in Blake's work at Genano.

"Dad, you remember when we went to the display room at Genano?"

Blake set aside his newspaper, rather than merely fold it. "Yes, I remember that. It was a very memorable occasion."

"I've had reason to recall something that happened that day. We caught up with Rob Jennison, or he with us, and you both were talking about something called the "Crow" project."

Blake sat up straight and looked at his son. "That's a corporate matter, Dani. We're not supposed to talk about some things outside of work."

Dani smiled. "I know. Believe me I know. I've been reminded again and again about security matters and respecting the "need to know" about them." He leaned closer. "But this is important."

Blake looked thoughtful. He very seldom saw his son act as intense as this. "All right. Keep your voice low and tell me what you're concerned about."

"Your Crow project involves gene splicing, as opposed to using nanotechnology for genetic manipulation, right?" Dani looked his father steadily in the eyes. "Perhaps an early version?"

Blake smiled grimly. "I can neither confirm nor deny any allusions you make."

"Did you ever encounter the name, Selena Sanchez?"

"It's possible. I know I've seen a few names at least similar to that. We had some names show up as a result of an epidemic among a population of people we were studying some years ago."

Dani sat forward at the table. "Don't make an official inquiry. Let's just assume the worst and be totally paranoid in the matter. It's the only way to be safe." Dani went into the kitchen and returned with two glasses of iced tea.

"I'd be willing to wager her name showed on a deceased list. She's not, but she's also not out of danger." Dani took a sip of tea.

"I'm going to go totally out of bounds here and suggest you accept what I'm speculating as sufficiently believable to consider lives to be on the line, including yours, mine, and many other people." He took another long sip of his iced tea. "I believe your Mr. Rob Jennison is much more than he appears to be."

Blake collected his glass and sat back for a moment.

Dani looked around casually. "What do you think would happen if the primary custodian of a secret project reported complete failure and a shut-down of the project, but actually kept it going so that he would have the upper hand on giving advice about similar studies in the future?"

Blake studied the horizon a moment. "That could be a damn clever way to get ahead in the organization."

"Particularly if someone was actually a member of two secretive organizations, and he was playing them against each other?"

"That could be a possibility, I guess. I'm puzzled why anyone might take such a risk, or what they might hope to gain out of it."

Dani studied him for a moment. "Have you, in your many years of study and work at Genano, ever encountered a chimera?"

Blake practically flung himself back from the table. "What ever made you consider that?"

Dani sipped his tea calmly, radiating calmness. "I was just idly speculating one day, and I wondered why a man would work for years at a place like Genano, and not ever take advantage of what they might have to offer in the way of minor, very affordable enhancements – and then I thought about some few cursed people who might be constitutionally unable to do so." He looked up at his father. "Am I guessing right?"

Blake nodded just perceptibly. "It's possible. Some chimeric individuals have severe problems getting evenly moderated benefits from genetic manipulation. You think Rob may be such a case?"

Dani shrugged. "It could be, and it might give him a reason to resent other people without such a disadvantage. He seems to be very friendly to you, but if he has a problem like that, he would most likely be motivated to hate you more every time he sees you."

Blake looked at his son with a haunted expression.

Dani leaned forward. "Now is the time to be most careful. If we're wrong, it's simply a laughing matter. But if we're right, it could be deadly serious. A mistake now could cost lives."

Dani smiled, "This is way over my head. The real problem is that it may be way over your head too. If we report it to someone who reports to Mr. Jennison, people will die." He sipped his tea. "It could even be beyond our government levels, and get into foreign offices. I have no way of knowing, and I suspect you are pretty insulated yourself."

Dani simply looked into his father's eyes. "I've considered that we could kill him, but the problem with that is that they might start killing us back, so that's no help. We could maybe fix him, but he might not be sufficiently grateful for that to make a difference either."

"I'd say, 'I want my mommy!' but this one's going to be all yours, I'm afraid, Dad. At least you don't have to make a decision right away. But you will have to make a right decision."

Eventually, Dani picked up his glass and started away. Blake made a gesture, and Dani stopped to be embraced once more by his father. They hugged, and kissed. Dani observed that Blake had tears in his eyes.

His father said "Thank you!" softly as Dani departed into the kitchen.

* * *

Curiously, the general lock-down seemed to turn into a bit of a "slow-down" as the work on the electrostatic fusion generators, their factory, the rocket assembly in its protected enclosure, and even the many locations where Dani's tri-copters were being put together began to enjoy a glacial cooling in their excitement quotient. The public maintained interest, but the work seemed to get more difficult every day.

No matter, no matter. Stories began to be told about the adventures the intrepid explorers *were going to have*, and the public consumed them with appropriate enthusiasm.

Dani, and Lori, Roni and Anastasia, and of course their brave genius of a Captain, Malcolm, became familiar figures all over the globe, as their friendly stories got told to both younger and older audiences.

Particularly exciting were the encounters with some remarkable helicopter-like flying craft, which arrived somewhat miraculously within hours when natural disasters made their inconvenient presence felt. And somehow a lot of the attending mercy-givers and rescuers seemed to have familiar uniforms quite similar to those amusing Space Cadets.

* *

About the Author

Brian Hawthorne lives with his wife and two children in Maryland. One of those "quiet types" that you would never suspect.

As an avid reader and Science Fiction fan, he is following a prescription written by Dr. Isaac Asimov; that any reader, after long enough, will want to write. To that end, he writes for his own entertainment, and that of his readers. With creative exuberance, he tells of relationships, ingenious conveniences, and stubborn human behaviors.

www.ingramcontent.com/pod-product-compliance
Lightning Source LLC
Chambersburg PA
CBHW020444130626
46549CB00001B/298